I AM
because
LOVE IS

God as Verb

by John Chuchman

The author's other titles:
"Springtime in Autumn"
"Pebbles of Wisdom"
"Quest"
"Sunset Awakening"
"Journeying Through Life"
"I Love My Church, BUT OH MY GOD!"
"WE Are Church"
"Is God Laughing or Crying"
"Let's Hospice Our Church"
"SACRED QUEST
Growth Through Loss and Love"
"Spirituality and Spiritual Growth
Beyond Hierarchical Church"
"In Search of Spiritual Horizons"
and "Nailing Honey to a Tree"

Thanks

to the Creator
for
The Gift of Life
and
the numerous opportunities
to Love
and
Be Loved.

Dedication

This book is dedicated to
My beloved Friend, Teammate, Associate,
Karen Rose Schrauben,
at this moment undergoing treatment for
pancreatic cancer
which has spread to her liver.

Karen has been
Loving Agent of the Holy Spirit for me,
Inspiring, Encouraging, Supporting, Loving me
through all of our many ventures together.

Even in this most difficult part
of her life journey,
she continues to inspire all
with her wonderful attitude
and contagious laughter.

Karen Rose Schrauben,
God's Energizer Bunny.

Introduction

I keep saying
that
my last book
is
my last book.

I guess
the Holy Spirit
has other ideas,
because
I keep getting inspired

to keep on writing
and
sharing it
with others.

So be it.

Love, John

Metaphors of God

The Metaphors for the Divine,
for a Triune God,
that seem to be at work for me
now

are

Source of Love,
Revelation of Love,
Enactment of Love

and

Mind,
Heart,
Gut/Intuition,
(The Immanent God)

God as a Verb

True Christians are mystics.

Christian mystical experiences unite,
allowing me to begin to feel
connected with
part of,
united with,
aware of,
one with
something or some activity
larger than myself.

God is an experience.

Christian saints and mystics
have described this encounter with God
as putting on the Mind of Christ.
Christian literature includes such expressions
as
One with Christ,
Temple of the Holy Spirit,
the Body of Christ,
the Divine Indwelling,
Participants in the Divine Nature.

This is an understanding of
the non-duality of God
that begins for Christians with emptiness.
It is a way of understanding Christ
as the Incarnate Word.

"Let the same mind be in me
that was in Christ Jesus,
who, though he was in the form of God,
did not regard equality with God
as something to be exploited,
but emptied himself,
taking the form of a slave,
being born in human likeness."

This is an encouragement
to empty myself,
to become as servant to another,
and to enter into the fullness of my humanity
and my full human potential.

This practice of putting on the Mind of Christ
and emptying myself
is one way I, as Christian,
may come to understand Jesus.

The ideal of Christian life
is to lose one's own
self-centered identity
in the wider activity of the risen Christ-Spirit.
It is to step back
and let this Spirit live within us.

This stepping back or emptying myself
of myself
resonates with the Buddhist bodhisattva,
who develops universal compassion
and a spontaneous wish to attain
Buddhahood
(the state of perfect enlightenment)
not for his or her own sake
but for the benefit of all sentient beings.

It is also in the Bible:
"Likewise the Spirit helps us in our weakness;
for we do not know how to pray as we ought,
but that very Spirit intercedes with sighs
too deep for words.

And God, who searches the heart, knows
what is the mind of the Spirit,
because the Spirit intercedes for the saints
according to the will of God.

I am convinced that neither death,
nor life, nor angels,
nor rulers,
nor things present, nor things to come,
nor powers, nor height,
nor depth,
nor anything else in all creation,
will be able to separate us
from the love of God
in Christ Jesus our Lord."

Stepping back,
letting the Spirit live in me,
allowing the Spirit to pray in and through me,
practicing meditation
as a Sacrament of Silence,
emptying and letting go of myself,
all offer a way to nurture and grow
within myself
the graciousness of spirit
that God gives
to each of us
in ways that are known only to God.

This offers a path in which the mystery
and light of Christ
may become known through dialogue
and practice with other sacred traditions;
here the Holy Spirit of the Christian Trinity
becomes boundless,
without limitations,
infinite in love,
infinite in acceptance,
infinite in potential,
endless in compassion and wisdom.

God must act and pour into me
when I am ready;
in other words, when I am totally empty of self
and creatures.
So I try to stand still and remain
in a state of emptiness.

I try to discard the form
and be joined to the formless essence,
for the spiritual comfort of God is very subtle.

Only the hand that erases
can write the truth.

On the Buddhist side,
there is the experience of nirvana
or emptiness
and the related concept
of dependent origination
or arising.

God is best understood as
the Ground of Being,
translated more freely and more engagingly
as Inter-Being:
the interconnected state of things
that are constantly churning out
new connections, new possibilities,
new problems,
and new life.
Understanding God through relationships
is critical.

The source and power of our relationships
are driven by the presence of the Holy Spirit.

Behind and within all the different images and
symbols Christians use for God:
Creator,
Abba,
Redeemer,
Word,
Spirit,
**the most fundamental, the deepest truth
Christians can speak of God
is that God is the source and power of
relationships.**

God as a verb is the activity
of giving and receiving,
of knowing and loving,
of losing and finding,
of dying and living
that embraces and infuses all of us,
all of creation.

If I'm going to talk about God,
God is neither a noun nor an adjective.
God is a Verb!
God is much more an environment
in which I live and move
and have my being.

God is above all things,
through all things,
and in all things.

The more awake I am to this presence
and this mystery,
the more I come to know God is here
in this very moment,
in the eternal Now.
This is the central message of Jesus
when he teaches me that
his relationship with God is intimate,
eternal,
and within.

This presence above, through, and in
constantly calls me into relationships of
knowing and loving another
all through my life,
filling me with the deepest joy
when I empty myself for the sake of others,
seeing and finding myself in others.

This presence is what I feel
when I am loved and accepted,
when I love and accept others,
and when I open
and give of myself selflessly.

As it says in Scripture:
"And when the Pharisees
had demanded of Him
when the Kingdom of God should come,
He answered them and said,
'The Kingdom of God cometh
not with outward show.
Neither shall they say, 'Lo, it is here!'
or 'Lo, it is there!'
For behold, the Kingdom of God
is within you.'"

A better image of creation
might be a pouring forth of God,
an extension of God,
in which the Divine carries on
the divine activity
of interrelating in and with and through
creation.
This pouring forth of God is the engine
or fuel of creation,
but we as a People of God,
created in the Image of God,
are also a part of this pouring forth.
How this all works is also part of the mystery.

God as the Trinity is the silence and the stillness
before all things,
out of which all creation arises from
the nothingness and emptiness
that is without form and void,
an image taken from
the first chapter of Genesis
when there was nothing except God.
It is out of this nothingness (no-thing)
or emptiness
that we all arise.

The way of Christ
is a way that calls me to love others
unconditionally
with great compassion and loving-kindness.

This is a call that I have tried to answer
by loving others
in all their diversity of beliefs and ethnicity,
even in all their suffering,
and in showing them through that love
how Christ lives and dwells
within my own being.

Jesus is not the way that excludes,
overpowers,
demeans other ways;
rather he is the way that opens us to,
connects us with,
and calls us to relate to other ways
in a process that can best be described as
dialogue,
now shunned by many institutional religions.

If Jesus really is the Way
that is open to other Ways,
then dialogue with other religions
and other believers,
should be part of what it means
to be a Christian.

As many Asian bishops and theologians
are saying today,
Dialogue is a new way of being in church.

Today I am called to be religious
inter-religiously.
Committed to Jesus and the Gospel,
I must also be open to other religions and
believers.

As a Christian,
someone grounded in Christ
and intimately involved
in this interfaith dialogue,
I am learning to value the truth
and teachings of other faiths
while sharing my own,
another way I feel embraced by
the risen Christ
while encountering the Holy Spirit
at work in the world.

God and Jesus for Me

(Inspired by a day with Bishop Spong in Tempe, Arizona)

What does the idea God mean to me?
Is God beyond religion?
Have I created God
In my own Image?

A theistic God
is one that answers my prayers,
fills my needs.
It is a god
that athletes use to succeed,
that politicians use
to sanction their actions.

How do I escape
the boundaries of religion,
to get a sense of True God?
If my prayers are not answered,
if my needs are not met,
Is my god
immoral? impotent?
uncaring?
How do I find a way to move beyond
my human view of God,
beyond Theism?

In the 3.8 billion years of life on earth,
my family of humans appeared
only 250,000 years ago
(though human-like creatures
roamed the earth
beginning 4 million years ago)

The gift/burden we've been given
is self-consciousness.
No creatures before us
were ever-self conscious.
None had an idea of the past;
None had thoughts of the future;
None asked about their purpose in life.

No creatures before us
thought about their death.

All simply lived as part of creation,
connected to all.
None felt alone
or separate from or unique
in Creation.
None experienced the anxiety
of self-consciousness,
the anxiety of living
and knowing *I am going to die.*

None wondered as I do,
Why I'm here.

I, as all humans,
live in the trauma of self-consciousness
and that takes
Courage.

Have I used religion to Cope
with this anxiety?
Religion seems a coping mechanism
for us humans
with self-consciousness.
Has my religion enabled me to cope
with the human anxiety
of knowing I am to die?

Has religion helped me find purpose in life
beyond myself?

Human beings throughout our history
seemed to have created religion(s)
to serve our needs,
to help us cope.
Religion seems to be a human creation
to manipulate *God.*

We've used ancient ideas of a Spirit World
just beyond us,
gods and goddesses of fertility
as well as male gods who would
judge and defeat our enemies
while protecting us.

The gods we've created to serve our needs
generally have been viewed as
External,
Invisible,
Available,
All-powerful,
Needy of our praise,
Needing to be pleased,
Helpful.
The gods we have created are
Everywhere (omnipresent,)
All-powerful (omnipotent,)
All-knowing (omniscient,)
Eternal (infinite,)

All we are NOT.

They help us to Cope!
God gives us purpose
helps ease our anxiety.

I have grown up with a God
(as has much of humanity)
that needed to be PROPERLY worshiped,
and that needed for me
to fulfill God's Will for me
(purpose.)

I have grown up
(as has much of humanity)
trying to win God's approval by flattery,
putting myself down
as a wretched sinner,
and following what I thought was
God's Will for me.
The God of my creation,
the God of human creation,
the God of mankind's religions
is
a Consciousness SEPARATE from me.

I think it's time I grow up.
I don't need to be *born again,*
I need to
Mature.

The security
found in religious fundamentalism
is an escape from reality.

23

I need to mature in it, not escape from it.

*I am a part of God
and always have been.
I am a part of a God of Universal
Consciousness,
part of One single Unfolding Whole.*

A touch of the Divine is in me.

I do not have a relationship with God,

I AM a relationship OF God.
God is the source of all life
flowing through the universe
of which I am a part.

A religion must allow that Divinity within me
to grow.

I sense
that worshiping God entails
**Living Life Fully Awake, Aware, Alive,
in the Precious Present Moment,
by Loving All Constantly,
and by striving to be
Who God Created Me to Be.**

There seems to be many pathways
to God,
with mine being the Experiences
of my own life.

The Divine Call
seems not to make me religious,
but instead,
to help me be *Fully Human*.
*I cannot glorify God
by denigrating myself, my humanity.
I am not wretched;*

I am a beautiful Creation of God.

I do not want a religion
that removes the anxiety of self-consciousness
which is reality.
I want a religion that gives me the Courage
to embrace reality.

Each religion seems like a well
seeking the Living Waters of the Divine.

Each is different,
but if they go *deep enough*,
they tap into the same Universal Source
Water of Life.

So how does my idea of Jesus
fit into this nontheistic view
of the Divine?

Jesus seemed to worship God
by being fully aware, awake, alive
in the present moment,
by loving all constantly,
(even those nailing him to the cross)
and by having the courage to be
Who He was created to be.

I know we really cannot talk about God
adequately.
God defies human description.
We can only really talk about
Our Experiences of God.

Our experiences in life live on,
but our perceptions and explanations
of life's experiences
can change.

An epileptic seizure was *explained* Biblically
in a way far different than it is today.

The New Testament
is not one book;
It is 27 different books
written during the period from 50 to 135 AD,
at least 21 years after Jesus' death.
They were not all written at the same time.

Paul's was the first, written around the years
51-64 AD.
He said, *God was in Christ*.
(Explanations of that abound.)
Paul said God is in Christ *at Resurrection.*

Mark's book (70-72 AD)
describes God descending on Jesus
at his Baptism in the Jordan.
Jesus Humanity was not Compromised.
It was an ecstatic experience.

Mark knew nothing of a Virgin Birth.

(Jesus' mother and her 4 sons and 2
daughters
thought Jesus was out of his mind.)

Mark writes of a risen Jesus
appearing to no one.
Jesus was raised *into a Life in God.*

Mark was the first ever
to ascribe miracles to Jesus.
There was no writing or evidence of miracles
before Mark,
not in the gospel of Thomas
or the Q writings.
Miracles were not original to the Jesus story.
Mark seems to have wrapped
the miracle stories of Moses, Elijah, and Elisha
around Jesus
using Isaiah's
the blind will see,
the deaf will hear, etc.

In the 9th Decade AD,
Matthew tells the Virgin Birth Story.
Surprisingly,
his long intro genealogy
includes four (4) women—unheard of!

Women were non-entities of the time,
simple containers for men's seeds.
Why were women included in Matthew's
genealogy?

Even more surprising is that
all four women were sexually compromised.

Was Matthew trying to respond to rumors
that Jesus may have been illegitimate?
Was he trying to show that God works among
us
even through our misdeeds?
Was the Virgin Birth story created
to protect Jesus' reputation?

Where did Isaiah prophecy a Virgin Birth?

Even Later,
Luke changed the wise-men, magi
into shepherds.
He changed the star at Bethlehem
into an angelic host.
Luke takes Joseph out of the picture
and emphasizes Mary.
(Joseph being told by an angel in a dream
is lost in favor of Mary being told directly.)

Luke adds Jesus' appearances
after resurrection,
walking, talking, eating, teaching,
having his flesh felt to prove his resurrection.

Luke adds the Ascension story
lest Jesus be walking the earth forever.
(Paul had no knowledge of an Ascension,
spoke of *Transformation*.)

Finally, John, 60 years after the death of Jesus,
dismisses the Virgin Birth Story
and writes that
God enters Jesus from *Eternity*,
from *Creation*,
The Word Enfleshed.

The Council of Nicea 325 AD
resolved the dispute about Jesus' Divinity
by proclaiming Him
Human AND Divine
leaving little room for Jesus' Humanity
in our thinking of Him.
On the cross,
Mark and Matthew's Jesus
seems very Human,
My God, My God,
Why have You forsaken me?
Luke's Jesus seems a little more Divine,
Into Your hands, I commend my Spirit.

John's Jesus, seems fully Divine from the cross,
It is finished
(the work of the new creation.)
Jesus experiences were *Real.*
The experiences of those
who encountered Jesus
were *Real.*

The explanations and perceptions of those
experiences
changed over time
and are changing over time.

In the 4th century AD,
Augustine proclaimed that
humans were infected with sin
and that the gates of heaven
were closed to us,
opened by Jesus' death on the cross
and that since salvation can only come
from God,
Jesus is God.

To this day,
liturgies in many religions
are re-enactments of the crucifixion of Jesus,
a *Sacrifice* of the Mass.

I cannot really believe in an all-loving God
who demands a human sacrifice
to appease God?
Guilt pervades all bad theology.
Adherents go through life
feeling responsible for the death of Jesus.

Scripture has been used
to defend the divine right of kings,
unsuccessfully;
to defend slavery,
unsuccessfully.
Scripture has been used
to defend discrimination of women,
unsuccessfully;
to defend discrimination of gays,
unsuccessfully.

I am not responsible for Jesus death!
I do not have to live my life in unworthiness
and Guilt.
Hierarchists have tried to control me
by telling me How I must Worship My Creator.
I reject the terms
redeemer, savior;
I am not wretched!
I am worthy to receive Him.

Jesus showed me
how to love myself enough
to become *Truly Loving.*

Jesus was fully alive, awake, aware
in the present moment;
Jesus was totally Loving of all;
Jesus was free to be
Who He was created to be;
He was Free to give his life away;
Jesus brought God to all with whom He
connected.

Nothing I can do
will remove God's Love of me.
Nothing I can do
will increase God's love of me.

Jesus demonstrated that Love.
Humanity has been set free!

As shown in the Acts of the Apostles,
the Holy Spirit descending on people
does not make them *religious;*
It sets them Free
to spread the Word
to the four corners of the earth.

Human Life could not birth
the God-Experience of Jesus.
Jesus introduced us to
The God Experience.

I need to recover that Experience
and in the process
bring God to all
with whom I connect.

I vow to bear witness to My Truth
staying open to other ideas
while being willing to change.
I wish to share my pearls of Wisdom
with others
while being gifted with their pearls of Wisdom.

If horses had a god,
t'would be a horse.
How can a horse envision more?
How can I envision God as God?

I must move beyond the god
created by religions
in my image.

All the Wrong Places

A Beautiful Creation
of the Divine,
why have I been looking for validation
in all the wrong places?

I have too long followed the lead
of my Ego,
directing me to look for
approval, reinforcement, acceptance
Outside myself.

I have too long been driven
to search for
Power and Control,
Affection and Esteem,
Safety and Security
Outside myself,
all of which are insatiable addictions.

All the while,
the real source of Validation
is my relationship
with my Creator
that spark of Divine
deep within me.

Too long have I been looking to others,
to organizations and religion,
to empty rituals, rites, and practices,
to affirm me
when
to my Creator
I need no validation or affirmation.

The Power and Control I sought
is only with the Creator of the Universe;
The affection I craved
is the Unconditional Love
of my Mother/Father God;
The safety and Security I tried to build
rest only with the Divine
to Whom I will return.

True Self

BEING HUMAN
provides me with a unique relationship
to time:
I am not confined to the relentless march
of my body
through linear time,
but am able to remember the past,
foresee the future,
and contemplate possibilities.

I can look at a tree
and see planks and beams
and a bridge,
look at mud and see adobe bricks
and a house.
I can create, repair, and maintain
to a degree and with a flexibility
unknown to other creatures.

This capacity of human consciousness
is evident in all human artifacts,
and whether ultimately it will serve
to replenish the earth
or to destroy it
is still in the balance.

But it is possible that my awareness
has a purpose
on another level as well.
Some religious and mystical teachings
hold that human consciousness,
in reflecting reality,
also helps to bring it into being.

According to an Islamic mystic, I act
"as the eye through which
God can see creation:"

"God praises me
by manifesting my perfections
and creating me in God's form,
And I praise God
by manifesting God's perfections
and obeying God."

How can God be independent
when I help and aid God?
Because the Divine attributes
derive the possibility of manifestation
from their human correlates.

"For that cause God
brought me into existence.
And I know God and bring God into existence
in my knowledge
and in my contemplation of God."

So perhaps, in an as yet unclear fashion,
I am part of
a great cosmic ecology of consciousness,
maintaining the form of the universe
against the impact of linear time,
because of my potential capacity
for metabolizing form,
made possible by my flexible
and encompassing relationship
to time itself.

In this process, I become part of everything
on a conscious level,
just as I am part of everything
on the level of gross materiality.

Just as my body is made up of atoms
that once were created in supernovae,
and passed through
a variety of inorganic and organic entities,
the material of my inner life consists of all my
perceptions
of other beings,
of earth,
sea,
sky,
and stars,
and of the fundamental laws that govern it all
and I am thereby connected to everything
on both levels,
and to the Whole,
the Source.

God through Whom I see, taste, smell, feel,
hear, enjoy, know everything,
is True Self.
Knowing That by Which I perceive both
dream states and waking states,
the great, omnipresent True Self,
I move beyond sorrow.

Knowing that my True Self,
is the universal Self,
maker of past and future,
I know I have nothing to fear.

In meditation,
entering the secret place of the heart,
God looks forth through beings.
That is True Self.

The boundless power, source of every power,
manifesting itself as life,
entering every heart,
born with the beings,
is True Self.

THE KEY QUESTION
is not what to do
but how to see.

Seeing is the most important thing,
the act of seeing.

I had to learn that it is truly an act,
an action that brings something entirely new,
a new possibility of vision,
certainty,
and knowledge.

This possibility appears during the act itself
and disappears as soon as the seeing stops.

It is only in this act of seeing
that I find a certain freedom.
So long as I had not seen the nature
and movement of the mind,
there was little sense in believing
that I could be free of it.
I have been a slave to my mechanical
thoughts.
This is a fact.
It is not the thoughts themselves
that have enslaved me
but my attachment to them.

I needed to see the illusion
of words and ideas,
and the fear of my thinking mind
to be alone and empty
without the support of anything known.
It was necessary to live this slavery as a fact,
moment after moment,
without escaping from it.

But then, I began to perceive a new way
of seeing.

Seeing did not come from thinking.
It came from the shock at the moment when,
feeling an urgency to know what is true,
I suddenly realized that
my thinking mind cannot perceive reality.

To understand what I really am
at any moment,
I needed sincerity and humility,
and an unmasked exposure
that I did not know.

This meant refusing nothing,
excluding nothing,
and entering into the experience of
discovering
what I thought,
what I sensed,
what I wished,
all at the very moment.

My conditioned thought
always wanted an answer.
What was important for me
was to develop
another thinking,
a vision.

For this I had to liberate a certain energy
that was beyond usual thought.

I needed to experience
"I do not know"
without seeking an answer,
abandoning everything
to enter the unknown.

It was no longer my same mind.
My mind engaged in a new way.
I saw without any preconceived idea,
without choice.

I chose to relax in not knowing why.
I learned to purify my power of vision,
not by turning away from the undesirable
or toward what is agreeable.

I learned to stay in front and see clearly.
All things have the same importance,
and I became fixed on nothing.

Everything depends on this vision,
on a look that comes
not from any command
of my thought
but from a feeling of urgency to know.

Perception, real vision, came in the interval
between the old response
and the new response
to the reception of an impression.
The old response was based on material
inscribed in my memory.

With the new response, free from the past,
my brain remained open,
receptive,
in an attitude of respect.

It is a new brain, different cells
and a new intelligence.
When I saw that my thought is incapable
of understanding,
that its movement brought nothing,
I was open to the sense of the cosmic,
beyond the realm of human perception.

Silent Spirit Within (SS)

The Spirit within is silent.
It is not talking or thinking about
what I am doing,
but it is aware of what I am doing.

I can be absorbed in a book
and be absolutely unaware of
my posture or the sensations of my body
because I am lost in the book.
If I call attention to that,
I become aware of the posture and the
sensations which are there all the time.

My Silent Spirit (SS) pays attention
to what goes on in my centers:
to what goes on in my head,
to what goes on in my heart,
to what goes on in my body.
It simply pays attention.

It's like listening to music.
I don't have to manipulate the impressions I
receive from music;
I just receive them.

This SS just receives impressions
from my behavior.

47

She hears my voice,
both my inner and my outer voice;
she is aware of what happens in me.
It is not thinking or internally talking
about what's going on in me.
It's simply being aware,
as though each function
had a mirror placed in front of it.

Experiencing the SS may not be exactly the
same thing with everybody.
We're all trying to do the same thing,
to have a SS whose function is just t
o be aware,
but it may be different for different people.

It does not seem helpful to put any words to it.
I could do that,
but it wouldn't make me any wiser.

The thing I try to do is
gain more experience of it,
to find how it feels different from
the ordinary condition
when my thoughts are experienced as "I,"
when my feelings are experienced as "I,"
when my body is experienced as "I."

I have a hard time differentiating the SS
from my mind.
But if I don't do that,
I cannot understand what the SS is.

In the ordinary way, I live in the state which is
called "identification."
This means that I feel myself to be my
functions.
It may be a thought,
it may be a feeling,
it may be a sensation,
but it is felt to be myself.

I am hammering a nail,
I hammer my finger
"Oh, I hurt myself."

Or I become angry and say,
"I am angry,"
instead of saying,
"Anger is rising in me."

And the SS is exactly something that is
not a function:
not a thought,
not a feeling,
not a sensation.

One of the great difficulties
of maintaining this special kind of attention
is that when I, for a moment
am aware of something,
I immediately start thinking about it,
judging it,
or whatever.

And my sense of myself slips into these
feelings,
these judgments of it,
and I am lost.
The SS is no longer there for me.

It is very difficult to realize for myself
that this isn't a thinking effort.
It is a naked awareness.

It isn't thinking about myself.
When I talk about being drawn
back into myself,
I am being drawn back into thought
about myself,
which is not the same thing at all.

I am tempted the whole time
to react to what I observe,
but the moment I do that
I am no longer observing.
It is extremely difficult not to react.
Something immediately begins
to think about it
and a running commentary sets up,
or I am pleased that I have noticed
something,
or I am disgusted with what I have seen,
or whatever.

These reactions draw my attention away from
the naked experience of myself.
What is the SS?
I don't think it's very useful
to give a verbal label of some kind.
What is important is to know
the difference in myself
between the times when it's there
and the times when it's not.

It is simply a witness at this stage,
a witness which is able to be a witness
because part of my attention
is in the witnessing.

It doesn't really help to label it.
What matters is that I experience it.
I feel the difference between the state
when something is separate
and looking on and experiencing,
and the state in which that is not there,
the state in which the candle is lit,
and in which the candle is out.

The SS can be considered to be
the germ of something that can in time
exercise some controlling influence
and bring some order
into the chaos of my psyche
if it grows in strength and grows in me.

It's not a thinking effort;
it's simply an effort of witnessing
what goes on in me.

The moment I think about it,
I'm not having the direct experience of it.

Think of the SS a naturalist
who is trying to observe
a rather elusive animal.

Most of the time,
I wish to learn to observe myself simply,
as I would a daisy or a butterfly,
without analysis,
without judgment,
without trying to understand the whys.

Before I can begin to understand the whys,
I need to observe simply,
because if I try to analyze as I go along,
it is mostly based on
my previous notions about myself.
I don't take in a pure impression
of what is happening.

My impressions are constantly affected
by my previous notions,
whether it is impressions of myself as I act
or whether it is impressions of other people.

So it is indeed desirable and necessary
to observe myself
with the same impartiality
as a naturalist observes a creature
he is trying to study
and to understand its habits.

But the trouble is,
it is very difficult to adopt the same stance
vis-à-vis myself
because always something in me feels
that I know myself
and finds it very difficult to look at
just what happens
and nothing else.

What happens, time and time again,
is that for a moment I can stand aside
and impersonally experience
what's happening,
but very quickly and imperceptibly
observation changes into comment,
and comment into emotional reaction
to what I have observed.

And the moment the observation changes
into comment,
I have lost the pure impression.

I will go on trying,
though it is not an easy thing to do.

This SS that observes has been likened
to a mirror
in which things are reflected;
a mirror doesn't have to move
to reflect movement.
It depends on how I understand the word
"observe."
This is the way I normally functions:
I observe and then something reacts.
When I try to observe myself directly,
it is almost impossible
to prevent some kind of feeling
or thought
about what I observe from arising in me;
but I have to keep the feeling or thought
about what I observe
quite separate from my act of observation.

The act of observation
sets off the emotional and intellectual centers
commenting, feeling,
and thinking
about what one has observed.

And it's very easy to get caught in the illusion
that this feeling and thinking about
what I have observed
is observation.

It isn't.
It's reaction.

And very often, when it sets up,
it catches my attention
so that my sense of myself goes into thinking,
and I ceases to have the SS.
I don't know if I am ever truly present,
especially when speaking.
Speaking is always difficult.
It's been recognized for centuries
as one of the most difficult things
because I identify with what I have to say.
So I will start with less difficult things
such as physical chores.

If I practice enough being present to myself
with simple things
that don't in themselves
make a demand on my mind or the emotions,
things that the body has learnt to do,
if I practice during those times feeling myself
separate from my actions,
then gradually, gradually
it may begin to become possible.

56

Before I am able to talk and remain
conscious of myself,
I can listen and remain conscious of myself;
it is not so difficult to listen as it is to talk.
And if I wish to stay present to myself
when I am talking,
I can use an anchor for the attention,
awareness of breathing or something like that,
which is quite possible to maintain
when I am listening,
but much more difficult
when I am speaking.

It's a question of practice
and of seeing these simple activities,
which are not important in themselves,
as practice grounds
where I can develop
the psychological muscles
which I will need
when things are more difficult.

I was just looking.

Seeing isn't what I thought it was.
What I called seeing was just looking.

I didn't see very much,
But I kept looking.
And that shifted my cognitive gears,
and there came a new moment.

The first look is a word, a name.
To me anything that is attached to words
is a mental looking.
Then, I began to look with my whole being
as if there were tentacles
that sensed and touched
the totality of the thing at which I was looking.

A tree stopped being leaves, branches, roots;
It started becoming a clustering,
a gathering,
a drooping,
a lifting,
a turning,
a teacher,
a friend.

Form me now,
seeing is opening a feeling
for the life of the thing I'm observing.
It's an understanding.

To me, the act of seeing is coming into
an understanding of
the whole of what's occurring.

So learning to see is learning to put together
my sight
with the rest of my Being,
which can take in a much larger view.

Seeing is really coming into contact with
what's there,
while just looking isn't really connecting
with what's there.

What are ways of knowing or receiving
what I'm observing?

A couple of things.
One is the word "attend,"
to wait.
Attention is to wait.

If I can wait with attention
with an openness,
I have a chance to really See.

I have to let go of
what I think something is supposed to look like
in order to see what it is.
That demands attending to it,
waiting,
allowing the impression to come in,
rather than going out to it.
It's a really subtle shift.

In seeing, I'm serving something
other than what I expect.
I'm not in charge.
In fact, I'm merely an objective bystander.
I'm just there
and it's moving through me,
and I'm not in the way.

When I can move down
to the almost metaphysical place
of our being here,
I simply witness.

I almost always had a vested interest
in the outcome of an idea
about how I wanted the world to be
or how I wanted myself to be
and, as a result,

I didn't see the world,
or myself.

So if I let go,
and I follow it,
there is a moment where this other kind of
reality becomes visible.
That's what I think seeing is.
My thoughts and desires were always
interfering,
but not always.

Here's the most shocking thing.
Often the largest silence I experience is in the
midst of noise.

All my ideas and the cacophony
actually pull (or push) something out of me.
This is where a quote from the Upanishads
is appropriate:

Like two golden birds in the self-same tree,
intimate friends,
the ego and the Self dwell in the same body.
While the former eats
the sweet and bitter fruits
of the tree of life,
the latter looks on in detachment.

Sometimes if I can keep mentally occupied,
my mind is so busy
trying to figure something out,
that something more essential comes out.

If there's so much cacophony,
it can bring up something so fierce
in terms of a desire be free,
it gives rise to a presence in the cacophony.
And the cacophony, like any good mouse
when I turn the light on,
disappears!

More than one part of me needs to see.
I can't see with my head alone,
I can't see with my heart alone,
I can't see with my eyes alone.

It takes all of me to truly See.

Notes

Hi,
I'm still in here.
I've been in here nearly 75 years.
Seventy-five years!
Oh, my.

My mind believes it;
seventy five earth orbits,
900 moon orbits,
three-quarters of a century!
My mind can perceive the facts.

It also knows
the machine is obsolescing,
showing wear and tear,
signs of the inevitable breakdown.

But my mind cannot absorb the 75 years,
bring them inside.
It only glues them onto
the thick crust of information scraps
it lugs about
on its surfaces.

No Surprise!
The longer I'm in here,
the more I get used to it.

The mind always has trouble
taking things compounded
out of time and space
with the most seriousness
because it, itself, as consciousness,
has been too little affected
by its prolonged exposure
to time and space.
At 75 years,
it feels the same as it did at 75 hours,
a sentient little glowing point of
me-here-knowing.

Always, everywhere,
it has stayed the same,
time-proof, space-proof,
same little glow
of me-here-knowing.
Why do I even try to describe it?
You know what I'm talking about,
it's Being,
Human-Being.

From In Here,
I am trying to slip out some Notes,
Notes from Being,
Notes from Human Being.

I will try to slip out a clear Note or two.

So many obstacles to doing so
make the task seem impossible;
so many thick layers of insulation
twixt us!

First, there's this fool
I room with,
prattling, sniveling, ego.
Even though I've stopped catering to it;
Even though I've grown sick and tired of it,
it continues to cling to me
like the overgrown infant it is.

Then there's the inadequacy of words,
worked, overworked to exhaustion
hauling so much garbage.

Slipping out a clear Note or two
seems impossible,
both for my head
and even for my feelings.

But thoughts and emotions
are not my All.
There's more to me.

There's one most crucial element
compounded into being
Human.

I don't know if there's a word
to describe it,
in Sanskrit, Mandarin, even Aramaic.

But it's not foreign,
It's Native, aboriginal native,
this critical element
in human-Being.

It is
IN HERE
with me.

This something else
assures me that
no matter what thoughts I may think
or what feelings I feel,
it IS possible
to pass clear Notes;
not only possible, but necessary,
an inborn organic need.

And so,
I proceed in Hope,
not in blind fuzzy faith,
but in firm solid knowledge.

After all,
over 75 years,
have I not received
tens of hundreds and thousands of
clear limpid Notes,
sent from near and far,
from the present and past,
from the living and the dead?

(My head interrupts.
It tries to provide rationale,
as it oft does after the fact,
as the well-intentioned organ that it is.)

Trouble is,
like a bug-collector
it kills everything
it pins down.
(But the effort is appreciated.)

And all these Notes,
no matter how diverse, how scattered,
are aimed at a single point,
The Point!
a point so close in, so obvious,
I keep overlooking it.

Instead of sticking to The Point
I have been so easily distracted,
wandering off.

But in this part of my life,
the distractions are losing their power
to divert me.
I have learned that the Creator
will not change the plans for the Cosmos
to suit me.

It finally dawns on me, too,
that my desire to reach the outer fringes,
my search for Horizons,
is only relative,
but that my need to reach
my utmost Center
is absolute.

I have lived in my Where and When
only relatively,
but I have lived
being human as a human-Being
Absolutely.

My existence
may belong to my time,
but I belong to my Being.

Even though I've amassed
lots of experiences
and many words to string together,
in hopes of sounding a clear Note or two,
I have no idea if I'll succeed.

But I am still here,
and I'm the one
I've been looking for.

Why me?
Because I'm the one Searching
and because the diversions
are no longer diverting me.

Because I have a Lack
and I am willing to acknowledge the Lack
to myself.

I refuse to hide My Lack,
to hide it from myself
or to hide in it.

I live with my Lack,
and my Lack lives within me.

And my Lack
keeps goading me,
keeps me searching,
but for what?

For something,
Something beyond everything,
everything so far, anyway.

So, my search goes on,
consciously, subconsciously,
sometimes sluggishly,
sometimes desperately,
looking for Something
to still my Lack.

I have discovered
that only one person can quiet my Lack,
the one using my mind, body, personality,
me, my human-Being.

I think
everyone is looking for the same Something
she/he lacks,
all to be found
in exactly the same spot.
I have been materialized
in order to experience
Human Life.
To have been incarnated as I have been
is miracle.
And so I stand in Awe
of Life,
beyond what I may think or do
moment by moment.

Beneath all my shifting emotions,
all my ideas and words,
beneath all my highs and lows,
I have found a foothold
on the bedrock of knowledge
knowing that I belong
Where and When I am
and that the Power,
the power that divides cells,
fires the stars,
twirls the planets
is the same Power
that fuels me.

I have been selected
To Be
and have just as much right to Be
as everything and anything else in existence.
Maybe even a shade more.

I have been created in the image of my Creator.

In what way?
Not in body.
Not in mind.
Infinity can't cram itself into a body or mind.

The real likeness
goes deeper than form or ideas.
What the Creator gave us was
the Gift of Creativity itself,
something more than all other species.

The Creator gifted us with
a strictly measured amount of Creativity,
enough to live a life
on an extraordinary level of existence,
the level I am living
right now.

What other hairy mammal
can distill ideas out of events?
What other primate
journeys inward as well as out?

What other creature
can balance
a vivid sense of potential perfection
against an even keener sense
of actual imperfection?

What other species
plays such a role
in the process of its own evolution,
in the evolution of the whole enterprise?
Why do I forget this?
Why do I squander my inheritance?
I am a Child of the Source,
legitimate and favored,
albeit an infant.

Yes, as a Spiritual Infant
I have staggered and stumbled,
whined and piddled,
meanwhile always growing.

I am finally maturing
into a real Son of the Source.
I hold a tight grip onto this fact,
my simple glorious relationship
with the Creator.

The fact of this Relationship
unlocks the enigma of my condition,
my internal warfare
caused by being a mere mammal
gifted with a Super Consciousness,
a Human-Being.

The fact of my relationship with the Creator
turns horror into Wonder,
a curse into a Blessing
a carnival of fools into
a School of Souls.

I think every single Human-Being
has heard this Note,
albeit muffled, distant, unclear
and has responded
with restlessness,
responded with a needing, a missing,
a yearning for
the Something that is more than anything.

This needing,
is my Gift!

This Lack
is my Gain.
It is the Light for my Path.

The urge I sense
is an urge
to come into my own,
my own as a uniquely-endowed life form,
on this uniquely-endowed bit of cosmic dust.

I am invited to Transcendence.

(What other convention of cells, brief candle
of sentience,
has received such an invitation?)
I know I'm not obliged to accept it.
Many don't.
I'm free to say No.

I can refuse to evolve,
and thus would devolve,
the way infertile seed
rots back into the earth,
to simply decompose.

There's plenty of room among the species
to drop down from my Humanity.
I am biodegradable.

I know I could not evolve by myself,
no more than a seed could become a tree
without air, water, soil, and sun.

I have been planted here
and the blessings granted me
over 75 years
have reached me so constantly,
so variously,
I simply must evolve.

So where did this patch of light within me
come from?
God knows I did not fabricate it myself.

It came addressed to me,
was delivered to my mind and heart,
waiting for me to snare meaning out of
nowhere.

The gift was given me
from inside and out.
My hunger seemed sealed within,
but the nourishment comes from without.

It is sent through Creation/Nature
and other means.

In the inadequacy and inaccuracy of words,
I call everything that feeds and sustains
my self-realization, Notes.

The whole Universe
is passing Notes.

I have been addressed
by the stars and the clouds,
the sea and the earth,
the plants, animals, stones.

And yet,
the Notes clearest to me
are Notes from
Human-Beings,
including the Notes from me, inside,
from here to here.

Widening the Cracks and Un-focusing

I can be very observant and sensitive
to my own state
and that of others,
but this seems to be a faculty
that falls between the cracks.
The cracks are in the continuity
of my conceptual mind.

Working with my inner self
is really about widening the cracks
and going to another level of
understanding/experiencing.
My mind can generate its own momentum,
going from one thought to the next
and then the next.

There is nothing necessarily wrong with that
except
that if it becomes continuous and habitual,
I am no longer in touch with my source,
with the core of my being,
with my purpose or meaning.
I get in touch only when there is a crisis.
Being in touch with my inner self
is a way of cultivating intuition.

Intuition is normally something that happens
beyond my control,
but I can also set the stage for it.
I can invite intuitive knowing.

I have to be very patient and friendly
with myself
and with what is going on in me.
This is a kind of love.
It can be called Caring Feeling Presence.

I work to make the boundaries
between myself and others
very permeable because
my mind can be such an isolating
and separating force.

Each individual is unique
and I can't really know what the other is
experiencing,
although I can support the other
in knowing her/his own experience;
I can empathize.

Empathy is a form of love,
opening a space for another.
This is a way to become more loving.

It is like meditation in the sense that
I begin with myself;
I have to have subjective empathy first.

Then I can be more open and sensitive
to others,
less judgmental,
more curious,
more appreciative.

An important aspect of love,
as opposed to desire,
is appreciating rather than wanting
or needing.

it's a way of getting in touch with
the source of symbols
and the source of myths.
The whole point, in a way,
is to make fresh symbols
directly from my own experience.

But I don't just get in touch with my inner self.
I invite it to become clearer.

Focusing is not a very good term.
I actually start with something
that is very unclear and vague.

Focusing suggests a laser-like attention.
It's the opposite:
a very relaxed and spacious sense.
Un-focusing.

It is un-focusing so my True Self is invited
to come into focus.
The sensation is like a warm ball
in the center of my chest
radiating energy.

In this Resonating,
my True Self does become clearer
as it responds and says yes.
It becomes more vivid, more present.

Beyond resonating, there is Asking,
at which point I actually begin
to have a dialogue with myself,
as if it were its own person or my inner child.
I raise a question
and then, instead of thinking about it,
I just let the space open up
and see if that sparks anything from within.
That's where I can really get new information,
new learning,
new wisdom.

Loving Listening cultivates a sense of
interconnection
or compassion,
a way of being real.

Loving Listening is a way of reconnecting
with my inner life
and of becoming more available to others
at a deeper level.

Most conversation is a mutual conspiracy
to keep us on the surface.
I tend to fall into the same patterns,
becoming angry or depressed
over and over again.

Loving Listening is a way of developing
empathy,
of becoming gentle within myself.
I have had a very strong critical voice
judging and labeling others
as stupid or abusive or incompetent.
It's a basic impulse in most people.

I seek a new way to communicate,
beyond the old ideological divides.
I can definitely go beyond ideology,
beyond any fixed conceptual system.

Meditation is making friends with myself,
welcoming whatever arises,
bringing Love in its wake.

Love is instinctive attunement.
Love is a tremendous quality of appreciation.

Contemplation
may be a long loving look at What Is
while
Love
is deepening appreciation for What Is.

Strange Time of Life

As each day is experienced
approaching age 75,
there is less and less need for me
to accomplish, achieve, attain, accrue,
amass.

This part of life is to provide me
the opportunity
to simply discover and uncover
that which is within,
my True Self
in existence eternally.

This might appear to be
a simple peaceful part
of life's journey,
but it isn't,
at least not so far.

Indeed, it's an unsettling time for me.
It still seems like there's something
I am meant to do
. . . and I haven't the foggiest idea What.

Oh, all my time after retirement
from the world of Commerce
has been a best time of my life,
thoroughly enriching
and overflowing with Love,
but
something remains
and I know not what.

Yes, I do discover/uncover more and more
of my True Self within;
I do take advantage of each and every
opportunity given me
to Love
and Be Loved,
and yet . . .

Perhaps it's just that having been around for
well over
two and a third billion moments,
the remaining few I've got left
seem too too precious to waste
missing something I am destined for.

I don't know.

Time in Silence

In Meditation,
we can experience God's presence
within us,
closer than breathing,
closer even than consciousness.

It is a Relationship with God
and a way to foster that relationship.

It is Personal Prayer
and a movement beyond conversation
to Communion with God.

Some method of experiencing Silence daily
is needed.
It is *Heartfulness*
more than mindfulness.

Meditation is attentiveness.
a gentle loving attention
to God.

Meditation
can activate all the indwelling powers
of the Holy Spirit,
which our egos and our preoccupations
hide and hinder.

What can flow from Meditation
are
Joy, Peace, Kindness,
Gentleness, Patience, Self-Control,
and
the Courage to respond to
the spontaneous call of the Holy Spirit
that arises in each situation!

Meditation,
try it, you'll like it.

Self-Discovery

No one can keep me from
discovering/uncovering
my True Self,
except me.

Nothing can inhibit me from
finding who I was created to be
except my own lack of courage,
patience,
imagination.

My journey of Self-Discovery
is all mine
to walk or to avoid.

I must shed some things along the way
and cannot waste my precious time
lamenting any hurts, losses, setbacks or
missteps.
I must be willing to let go
of the masks I wore/roles I played
in the process of surviving
and establishing my identity.

The journey is not without pain and grief.

If I do not find True Self,
it is only my doing.

I know God always gives me exactly
what I truly need
so I DO deeply desire
my True Self, God, Goodness, Truth, and
Beauty
in Love.

Regaining Lost Myth

Myth
comes from the deep and collective
unconscious
of Humanity.

Myths are not true in particular,
but entirely True in general.

Myths are not historical fact,
but Spiritual Genius.

Myth
holds life and death,
the explainable and unexplainable
together as One.

Myth holds together the paradoxes
that the rational mind cannot process.

Myth, just like poetry,
makes unclear and confused emotions
brilliantly clear
and
Life Changing.

Sacred Myths
keep people healthy, happy, and whole,
even inside pain.
They pull us into
Deep Time (past, present, and future, all).

Myths are
Food for the Soul.

So, why do we discount Myth as untruth?
. . . try so hard to dispel Myths?
Why have we so little sense of Myth?
Might we be too mind-dominated?

God; For me, The Universal Poet

God became the Word,
A Word so clear, so evocative, so new,
that It can only be expressed poetically.

God is The Word the world has been seeking
since the beginning,
A Word which says it all,
A Word which has not been edited,
A Word which astounds.

As Poet, God creates everything anew.
The poetry of God is miracle,
turning death to life.

'This is my Body!' was a poem at eventide,
but since then, God belongs to the world
and can be eaten.

"Your sins are forgiven!" was a poem
in the heart of the night
but from then on the whiteness of snow
belongs to all seasons.

"This day you will be with me in paradise"
was a verse apart from time,
and since then the infinite and the eternal run
in our blood,
nourishing our hope.

As poet, God knows how to say the most
difficult and most astounding things
with the natural simplicity of a child.
As poet, God knows how to fill
the gloomiest things
with light,
warm the coldest things,
and bring hope even to eyes
that have been lowered in shame.

As poet, God brings music to everything
Divinely touched;
Everything, even wretchedness, miraculously
merits a poem.

Poet-God, gathers all the poetry
that was hidden in creation.
There does not exist a poem
which God has not already written,
recited and felt.

For God, everything is poetry:
a hen, a coin, a well, a grubby child,
a woman who loves,
a man who fears and doubts,
a woman in labor,
a fish laid on the burning embers at lakeside,
the austere asceticism of John the Baptizer
and the simple free spirit of his disciples
who did not fast.

God goes on being eternal poetry
as Eternal Word, resounding or silent.
Poet-God goes on being
the great Minstrel of history
in people's hearts.

God goes on being a poet
because in God there is only beauty,
sensitivity, tenderness, intelligence, prophecy,
and a passionate love
for everything that exists.

*Every true poet is in some way a revolutionary
because with his/her art
he/she delves into the heart of things:
she/he stirs the waters
and the hidden mud comes to the surface.*

Poet-God is history's true revolutionary.
Divine poetry is always up to date and vital.
Divine verses, words, are often a shock,
a goad,
an alarm bell.

Poet-God, my sensitive God, my revolutionary
God,
is difficult to accept for those who think about
God
in mathematical terms,
for those who cannot conceive of a God
enamored of tangible things,
for those who prefer a mute, impenetrable
and impassive God.

But God, for me, will always be Poet,
a Poet of the infinite and a Poet of the earth,
for my earth, to my dear earth.
God is sensitive to every vibration of living
poetry,
poetry of flesh and blood,
human poetry.

God, for me, is poetry personified.

Poet God is the inspiration
of every created being
who allows his heart to be filled every moment
with that mysterious Word
that keeps us in existence
and reminds us that
life is not absurd,
but truly Beauty-Full,
Poetically so!

Sacred Space

First Nation Peoples,
far from primitive,
gain experiential experience
of
Sacred Space
from an early age.

But,
not a First Nation Person,
I am where I am now
at this very moment
also in
Sacred Space.

My body
is Sacred ground
when I am aware of
the Presence filling it.

I don't know where *Awareness* comes from;
it is mystery.
But, here it is;
and with it
I gain respect for this *Inner Presence*
and my relationship
with the surroundings.

I used to think only of Holy Places
as being sacred,
generally in my mind alone.
The awareness and experience of being
a Sacred Creation of the Sacred Creator
involves my total being.

Where two or three are gathered . . .

Jesus buried in the tomb,
is buried in our hearts.
Jesus risen,
is risen in our lives and our actions.

The sign of Jesus' coming is
the Love in our lives
and the Spirit in our actions.

If we continue to live in fear,
we prevent Jesus from being born again
in us.

The Good News
is that the Second Coming
is Through Us.

When I let Jesus
be born again in me
through Love,
I am one with my Creator.

That Unity
brings peace, joy, and love.

Jesus replaced rules and regulations
with Love.
Rules and regulations do not bring us to God,
but in fact, keep us from God.
They may be the foundation for order,
but Love is the foundation for Life.

Those stuck in hierarchical rules and
regulations
end up with very unhappy lives.

Love is our essence.

Reality; Changed or Clarified

Jesus did not change reality;
He simply revealed it.

God did not need to redeem us;
but simply to remind us
that we have <u>Always</u> been
God's daughters and sons.

When our minds and hearts
can be open to this TRUTH,
we experience our own Resurrection.

When we live in this Divine Reality,
we proclaim the REAL Good News.

Jesus,
thus, delivers us
from our mistaken reality
as fallen unworthy humans,
and restores to consciousness
our *Divine Reality.*

*Don't you really want to help share
this REAL GOOD NEWS?*

It could change the world!

*Happiness comes
in being who we are,
Love and Truth.*

The *Real* Good News

St. Paul tells us
Jesus does not want sacrifice;
He wants Love,
because He IS Love.

The *Real* Good News
we should be spreading
is that

We do not need to be *Saved*

from anything

other than a belief
that we are solely human.

We were already *Saved*
when we were born,

saved from nothingness.

That is the Only *Salvation*
We will ever need,

except perhaps from Fear.

Our first priority is

to recognize our Divinity as a Child of God;

our second is

to Love and Be Loved.

So Spread the Good News!

Divine Presence

Did I really believe

that

God was more present

in

the Bread and Wine

than

in those of us

gathered to offer and consecrate it

in His Name?

Why would a hierarchy

wish to perpetuate

such a notion?

Peace and Thirst

My discovery,
thanks to Mother Theresa's *Simple Path*,
that
Peace is **not** rest,
not tranquility,
not restfulness,
but indeed,

Love in Action,

has helped me accept

that my thirst,
my Quest,
my searching and seeking

will ne'er be satisfied
in this life.

Peace is not
a matter of arriving,
. . . anywhere

or achieving or attaining
. . . anything.

If the true Life Journey/Quest
is one of Self-Discovery
and I exist only in relationship with my Creator,
there is no way
I can arrive at a fulfilled understanding
of Self
in this life.

OK.
I'm going to be content
just putting my Love in Action.

Entering the Now

The NOW
is not accessible by my mind.

My knowledge of what is happening
at any given moment of time,
conditioned by my cultural habits
and modes ot thought,

is inadequate
to what is actually occurring.
I am simply unaware
of much of what is occurring,
even within my own body.
And
I am rarely aware of the significance
of what is occurring.

I have often assigned a degree of
significance
to an event in my life,
only to discover later
a much different pattern.

Whenever I discovered
the inadequacy of my knowledge/mind,
I either excused it,
or forgot it.

109

I rarely addressed the inadequacy,
losing the chance to
enter into it,
feel it,
and address it.

Do I know what is really going on
in my own inner world?

Do I really know what is really going on
in the inner world of others?

What do I look like in the eyes of others?

What do I actually see
in the world around me?

When I take the time,
and make the effort
to acknowledge my vast and obscure
ignorance,
I learn
Deep Humility.

Doing so,
I am inspired to a new kind of initiative,
a reaching out
to All that is Other
toward a new kind of Awareness.
How ironic!

My becoming *Aware* of
the inadequacy of my mind/knowledge
leads me to
a more adequate awareness
of my true state.

A key, thus, for me
to being able to enter the Now
is the realization that my mind alone
provides inadequate knowledge,
that I must reach out to All that is Other in
Creation,
and in doing so
attain a greater self-awareness.

For the Creator,
Now is all that exists.
When I become more truly self-aware,
beyond the inadequacy of my knowledge,
seeing myself as one with the Creator,
I can enter Now.

All This Time and I Did Not Hear

As I look now
at this beautiful gift
of Creation,
I get a message.
It has been screaming at me
all of my very existence,
a message I knew
but did not know I knew.

There is not a single thing out there,
no tree, plant, bird, critter, rock,
that rues what happened in the past--
not last year, not last month, not yesterday,
not a minute or even a second ago.

There is not a single thing out there,
no bush, no flower, no rabbit, no spider,
no drop of water,
that worries about the future
or lives in angst
that someday it will cease to be.

All of Creation,
plants, animals, wind, clouds, rain, cacti, sun,
waves,
all of Mother Nature's (Mother God's)
Goodness
shouts out in Uproarious Simplicity
Just
Be!

Enough, mind of mine!

You have refused to let me just **Be.**
You constantly drag me back into the past
or pull me into the future,
neither of which exists.

**Creation is in neither of those places,
only in the Now.**

I'm taking Control
and am going to spend a great deal more of
my time
with the Original Blessing,
The Gift of Creation,
in the Precious Present Moment.

Life is full of Gifts,

Gifts for which I did not ask,
given me for some mysterious reason
I did not discover at first,
and perhaps never will.

These Gifts were not a matter
of choice
nor of my Quest.

My life has been one of learning
how to
Receive them.

It takes tremendous work
to learn how to use them
and they end up changing
who I am.

A birth, a death,
a joy, a sorrow,
have each been teaching me
how to receive the Gifts.

What seems to make the receiving of the Gifts
possible is
Trust,
Trust that my relationship with the Creator
is the most important thing,
with the content of the Gifts
secondary.

Before I know the content of the Gifts given
me,
I must be willing to receive them.

It is in the Trust that God and I are in Love
that I begin to learn the content of my Gifts,
enabling me to ask
in vulnerability
for what I need.

So I am given Gifts
for which I did not ask
and it is in the trust of receiving them,
learning them, and using them
that I am enabled to ask for the Gifts I need.

Love and Death

seem to have a common root.

Love triumphs over death
not because it abolishes death,
but because it is itself
of death.

In death is the surrender total
as it is with True Love.

In death, as in Love,
I am completely and utterly
exposed
without reserve.

In entering death,
I enter, not a strange land,
but, indeed,
an inner chamber of Love.

A resistance to death
is a resistance to Love
is a resistance *to Life*.

Giving Up of Self
seems an essential
of Death
and
of Love.

Thoughts about the formation or modification of

A Small Faith Group/Intentional Eucharistic Community

I offer these as possible characteristics:

Freedom of Thought
Sense of Community, Loving and Caring,
Supportive
Dialogue, not just discussion

Willingness to Search *Outside the Box,* outside
conventional thinking
Progressive, Evolutionary Theology
Ideas not boxed up and finished

Willingness to dwell in Questions/Ambiguity
Answers not mandatory, Live the Questions
Acceptance that Answers are *Within*

Full Group Participation
Social Interaction
Meals together

Forward Looking, not backwards
Adult Faith

Abandonment of need for security

New Ways of looking at things
Not all need agree
Acceptance of Unknowing

Desire for *Refueling/Recharging*
No Power issues,
Community of Equals
A *Living Tree*, not petrified forest

Creative Liturgy

Nourishing/Nurturing

Truly Catholic/Sacramental

Want to help start one?

The Divine,

which is Absolute,
is necessarily Infinite.

As such,
the Divine infinitely radiates itself
since no barriers can exist
to prevent
this infinite radiation.

The Divine
radiates itself
as the Universe
including
me.

But as One with the Divine,
I am more than just a devoted Lover
who longs to unite with God,
nor am I only
the valiant Seeker
who struggles to know the Divine.

For most of my life,
I dealt with the Divine
as One Apart
from me.

But I
as Lover
and
as Seeker
exist only as
Loved and Known
by the Creator,
not really
apart.

Creation,
my individual Soul,
and
God
are indeed one.

I can distinguish myself
from others
for purposes of communication
but
my mind, heart, will,
apart from God
do not really exist.

*It is not I who lives,
but Christ that lives in me.*

This is not simply
identifying myself with God,
it is the honest recognition
that
the Divine exists alone
and that
all of the universe,
all of creation,
including me,
is simply
the radiation of that

Eternal Infinite.

Connecting with One in the Midst of Grief

When I am about trying to help one
experiencing a loss in life,

The chase and the hiding is a time of hopes
and fears
for both of us,

The untangling and understanding
of the Life/Death/Life aspects of
the relationship brings forth compassion for
the task,

As we relax into trust,
we gain the ability to rest in the presence and
goodwill of each other,

We each share both future dreams
and past sadness,
Our hearts eventually sing up new life,
Our bodies, minds, and souls intermingle,
We discover each other as a kind of spiritual
treasure,
and
We become one.

We become one,
not only with each other,
but with all of humanity,
and with

God.

From the Hopi

It is time to speak your Truth.

Create Community.
Be Good to each Other.
Do not look outside yourself for the Leader.

This is a Good Time.
This is the Hour.

The River is flowing very fast.
It is great and swift and some are afraid.
Some try to hold on to the shore.

The River has its destination.

Let go of the shore; push off into the middle of
the River.
Keep your eyes and heart open
and head above water.

See who is in the River with you.
Help each other and Celebrate!

Take nothing personally,
least of all yourself.

The time of the Lone Wolf is over.

Gather!

All that we do now must be done
in a Sacred Manner
and in Celebration.

We are the ones
We have been awaiting.

The Sacred Secular Sacred

In this time of rapid change
and my own deep thinking,
I hold on to the conviction
I am an integral part of the great chain
of Being.

My human consciousness
evidences this for me.

I stand in awe of
and reverence for
the unpredictability of life,
the sacredness of it.

I don't think that
religion has a monopoly on the Sacred.
One does not have to be inside
a church building
or to witness something
which a cleric administers.

Even the Dalai Lama
is calling for a more secular less-religious
spirituality.

Life is amazingly creative
and
surprising,
not simply derived from Biology or Physics.

Laws of science
can never predict the emergence of life.
The creativity of life
evidences
the True, the Beautiful, the Good.

Being in the world
is not merely cognitive for me,
but the full integration of my
humanity, imagination, inventiveness, thinking,
feeling, intuition, sensing, emotions,
and whatever else I bring to the party.
My vision
is that both science and religion
seek and reflect the sacred.
My Vision
is that all of creation,
including me,
is
One with the Creator
and thus,
truly
Sacred.

Non-Path

those that know me
have heard me speak of
my Spiritual Quest
as a Path,
a path up the mountain of life.

I thought
that there is a way I should be,
a relationship I should have with my Creator,
such that my progressing
from here to there
involved taking
a Path.

Meister Eckhart wrote
that Spiritual Growth is not a journey,
but that if it is,
it's a journey of a millimeter in distance
and *several hundred miles deep.*

So, was my Path metaphor wrong?

How could I move from illusion to reality
without granting my illusion a reality
of its own?

How could I conceive of reality as elsewhere
without casting a veil over it, here and now?

Zen Masters
say that in order to be enlightened,
one must be enlightened.

William Blake conceives the Spiritual Path,
not as the attainment of some distant Truth,
but the removal of
the tendencies, passions, intellectualizations,
and distractions
which prevent us from realizing our present
identity as one with that Truth we seek.

Maybe paths go nowhere,
maybe paths end exactly where I stop.

But even though I am in essence
one with my Creator now,
my lack of full awareness and appreciation
of that reality
tells me that work remains to be done.

The work may be illusory in an absolute sense,
but nonetheless, necessary.

I know I cannot concentrate on the means
alone
else I'm left with nothing but abstraction.

It seems that any Spiritual Growth
depends on my realization
that God is the Doer, not I,
and that no one walks a Spiritual Path.

It seems that the Spiritual Path
is simply an ongoing dialogue
between any of my efforts
and the Generosity and Grace of my Creator.

The relationship
of my efforts
to the Grace of God
perhaps is best described as
the state
of my growth **IN** God.

So, if my Quest
is to change
from climbing a path up the mountain of life
to one of Dialogue with my Creator
by removing the blinders
to my present Oneness with the Divine,
how do I proceed?

Grace

I never started out, nor ever dreamt,
to be a spiritual guide or emotional
companion
for those experiencing Grief on life's journey.

It has been pure Grace.

It came about because I was given
the immense privilege and gift
of being taken inside the lives
of the countless people I have met
in my Grief and Spiritual Growth Ministries.

What brought us into kinship
was the discovered God-given ability
to travel inward,
to connect the inner experience
with the outer experience,
and to trust that the Divine
is found in all of Life's experiences.

The willingness to be *open to Growth*,
to keep *climbing the Mountain of Life*,
to give self over to
Transformation
by continual *Attentiveness* to
the movement of the *Holy Spirit* in our lives
has helped many of my fellow travelers
and
in the process,

me.

No Longer

(Bishop Spong)

I will no longer debate the issue of
homosexuality
in the church with anyone.
I will no longer engage the biblical ignorance
that emanates
from so many right-wing Christians
about how the Bible condemns
homosexuality,
as if that point of view still has any credibility.

I will no longer discuss with them
or listen to them tell me
how homosexuality is
"an abomination to God,"
about how homosexuality is
a "chosen lifestyle,"
or about how through prayer
and "spiritual counseling"
homosexual persons can be "cured."

Those arguments are no longer worthy of my
time
or energy.

I will no longer dignify by listening
to the thoughts of those
who advocate "reparative therapy,"
as if homosexual persons
are somehow broken
and need to be repaired.

I will no longer talk to those who believe
that the unity of the church can
or should be achieved
by rejecting the presence of,
or at least at the expense of,
gay and lesbian people.

I will no longer take the time to refute
the unlearned and undocumented claims of
certain world religious leaders
who call homosexuality "deviant."

I will no longer listen
to that pious sentimentality
that certain Christian leaders
continue to employ,
which suggests some version of that strange
and overtly dishonest phrase that
"we love the sinner but hate the sin."

That statement is nothing more than
a self-serving *lie*
designed to cover the fact that
these people hate homosexual persons
and fear homosexuality itself,
but somehow know
that hatred is incompatible
with the Christ
they claim to profess,
so they adopt this face-saving
and absolutely false statement.

I will no longer temper
my understanding of truth
in order to pretend
that I have even a tiny smidgen of respect
for the appalling negativity
that continues to emanate
from religious circles
where the church has for centuries
conveniently perfumed
its ongoing prejudices against blacks, Jews,
women and homosexual persons
with what it assumes is
"high-sounding, pious rhetoric."

The day for that mentality
has quite simply come to an end for me.
I will personally neither tolerate it
nor listen to it any longer.

The world has moved on,
leaving these elements
of the Christian Church
that cannot adjust
to new knowledge or a new consciousness
lost in a sea of their own irrelevance.

They no longer talk to anyone
but themselves.
I will no longer seek to slow down
the witness to inclusiveness
by pretending that there is
some middle ground
between prejudice and oppression.
There isn't.

Justice postponed is justice denied.
That can be a resting place
no longer for anyone.

An old civil rights song proclaimed that
the only choice awaiting
those who cannot adjust
to a new understanding
was to "Roll on over or we'll roll on over you!"
Time waits for no one.

It is time for the media to announce that
there are no longer two sides
to the issue of full humanity
for gay and lesbian people.
There is no way that justice
for homosexual people
can be compromised any longer.

I will no longer act as if the Papal office
is to be respected
if the present occupant of that office
is either not willing or not able
to inform and educate himself on public issues
on which he dares to speak
with embarrassing ineptitude.

I see no way that ignorance and truth
can be placed side by side,
nor do I believe that evil is somehow less evil
if the Bible is quoted to justify it.

It is time to move on.
The battle is over.
The victory has been won.
There is no reasonable doubt
as to what the final outcome
of this struggle will be.

Homosexual people will be accepted
as equal, full human beings,
who have a legitimate claim on every right
that both church and society have to offer
any of us.
Homosexual marriages will become legal,
recognized by the state
and pronounced holy by the church.

Can any of us imagine
having a public referendum
on whether slavery should continue,
whether segregation should be dismantled,
whether voting privileges should be offered to
women?

I will also no longer act as if I need
a majority vote of some ecclesiastical body
in order to bless, ordain, recognize and
celebrate the lives and gifts
of gay and lesbian people
in the life of the church.

No one should ever again be forced
to submit the privilege of citizenship
in this nation
or membership in the Christian Church
to the will of a majority vote.

The battle in both our culture and our church
to rid our souls of this dying prejudice
is finished.
A new consciousness has arisen.
A decision has quite clearly been made.

Inequality for gay and lesbian people
is no longer a debatable issue
in either church or state.
Therefore, I will from this moment on
refuse to dignify
the continued public expression
of ignorant prejudice
by engaging it.
I do not tolerate racism or sexism any longer.

From this moment on,
I will no longer tolerate
our culture's various forms of homophobia.
I do not care who it is
who articulates these attitudes
or who tries to make them sound holy
with religious jargon.

Things do get settled and this issue
is now settled for me.
I do not debate any longer
with members of the "Flat Earth Society" either.
I do not debate with people
who think we should treat epilepsy
by casting demons out
of the epileptic person;
I do not waste time engaging
those medical opinions
that suggest that bleeding the patient
might release the infection.

I am tired of being embarrassed
by so much of my church's participation
in causes that are quite unworthy
of the Christ I serve
or the God whose mystery and wonder I
appreciate more each day.

141

Indeed I feel the Christian Church
should not only apologize,
but do public penance
for the way we have treated people of color,
women, adherents of other religions
and those we designated heretics,
as well as gay and lesbian people.

Life moves on.

As the poet James Russell Lowell once put it
more than a century ago:
"New occasions teach new duties,
Time makes ancient good uncouth."
I am ready now to claim the victory.
I will from now on assume it and live into it.
I am unwilling to argue about it
or to discuss it as if there are two equally valid,
competing positions any longer.
The day for that mentality has simply gone
forever.

No longer . . .

Without a Doubt, Faith?

You cannot be a wo/man of faith
unless you know how to doubt.

You cannot truly believe in God
unless you are capable of questioning
the authority of prejudice,
even though that prejudice may flow down
from some religious authority.

Faith is not blind conformity to a prejudice,
a "pre-judgment."

It is a decision,
a judgment that is fully and deliberately taken
in the light of a truth that cannot be proven.

Faith is not merely
the acceptance of a decision
that has been made by somebody else,
even a so-called *Magisterium*.

Beauty Within or/and Without

An associate and dearest friend suggested,
*John, so much of your poetry
is about your own inner journey/quest,
Write some more about
the Divine at Work in the World about us.*

I explained that
one reason I write in the First Person
is that I am sharing
my own journey,
my own experiences,
my own discoveries,
which might not apply to others.
I never want to sound
preachy
or imply in any way
that Others should follow my path.

In seeing all the Beauty around me
in the world
I think that it is inadequate to say,
Beauty is in the eye of the beholder.

I think it is Truer that
Beauty is in the *Soul* of the beholder.

When I am able to recognize the Beauty
all around me in the world,
as I oft do,
it is by virtue of my familiarity with it,
my sense of it,
my connectedness with it,
my oneness with it.

The Beauty in the world
all about me,
is both objective and subjective.
My awareness and appreciation of it
in fact,
bridges the gap between the two,
(Outer and Inner)
unveiling the Core
where the two are *One.*

The Beauty I see and appreciate
in the world all about me
and my own inner beauty
as a creation of the Divine
and Not opposed,
but really
to be understood as
one in the same.

The Greeks called it
Kalokagathia,
Beautiful Goodness
worthy of a deeply encompassing response.

The Beauty apprehended by my senses,
the inner beauty that echoes my most
profound humanity,
the supreme beauty of the Divine
all demand from me
all that I am and can be.

The non-realization or the non-acceptance
of my True Self
as a Beautiful Creation of the Divine
limits, restricts, impedes
an awareness and appreciation
of the Beauty of Creation
all about me.

Escape from the prison
of guilt and unworthiness
makes all of creation
that much more Beautiful,
subjectively
and, I believe,
in some mysterious way,
even Objectively.

146

A Non-noun God

St. Irenaeus of the second century
told us
We can never see God as an object,
only by sharing in
God's own self-understanding.

This self-understanding of God
is grounded in Love,
in Compassion,
in Loving Kindness
towards others, the world,
and ourselves.

Union with God
is union with one another,
with creation,
with the reality of God's Love.

It is Union without loss of personhood,
to unite without destruction of the Other,
the nature of True Love.

The Holy Spirit
works within us
helping us to grow,
in knowledge,
in Freedom,
In Love,
leading us to
our fullest potential.

Time

Time as an absolute
is just an illusion.

Time has no objective reality.

Time is a phenomenon of the mind.

I've been used to dividing time into
past, present, future.
But the present is truly elusive.
The moment I say, *now*, the nowness is gone.

Just when the sun is in the middle of the sky,
it is no longer in the middle of the sky.

But if the present is elusive and fuzzy,
so must be the past and future.

Even Jesus said,
. . . *before Abraham was, I am.*

During moments of intense Joy,
I am hardly aware of time.

Do Joy and time co-exist?

When one of my talks at a workshop or retreat
is going well
and I'm in sync with the audience,
I cannot believe how much time has passed.
On other occasions,
time seems to crawl at a snail's pace.

Time, thus, seems to speed up or slow down
based on my inner state.

What's eternity?
Is it a very long duration
of time?

Or is Eternity something apart from time?

Perhaps Eternity is in
the *Thoughtless Zone*
or if you prefer
the Thought-Free Zone.

Perhaps Spiritual Growth
is in ending the addiction
to the left brain.

Living in *a Thoughtless Zone*
might just be living in
a Timeless Zone.

150

The Kingdom of God,
Eternity,
might just be
living in the Thoughtless Zone,
the Timeless Zone.

Eternity
might just not be
the indefinite extension of time,
but perhaps

the disappearance of time.

Perhaps
The Kingdom of God
IS at hand.

Maybe it is NOT
a promise,
but a present reality.

Perhaps Anthony DeMello
had it right when asked the whereabouts
of heaven,
How do you explain to fish where the sea is.

Jesus said the Kingdom of God
is in the midst of you.
It cannot be sought
as we already have it.

The Kingdom, or Heaven,
is always a future event or place
for the left brain
which seems unable to dwell
in the present moment.

The Kingdom of God,
better yet, the Kindom of God
is not a matter of thought,
not a matter of place,
not a matter of time.

My desires
all need time,
all relate to the future.
If I could get to
the moment
where time disappears,
where there is no tomorrow,
all my desires
would disappear.

When I can be
truly aware of the moment,
there will be no time,
no thought.
I would be
in the Kindom.

A Path

I seek a different path
along life's journey,
an affirmative and friendly path
without condemnation.

I seek a path
that recognizes human limitations and
weaknesses
and accepts me as I am.

This path
is of the Kingdom of God
in the Here and Now,
not in some distance place or time.

The Path I seek
is not one of power and control,
having no need of those.

Movement along the path
requires only Love and Self-Abandonment
and
Living in the Moment.

Along this path I seek,
there is nothing to fight, suppress, condemn,
or reject
as Everything Belongs.
Nothing is secular;
Everything is Sacred.

I realize that this path
goes against everything that
traditional religions teach.
While they wish to suppress my passions,
this path requires that I use my passions
for Enlightenment.

On this Path,
instead of having to fight my passions,
I will be able to harness them
for Self-Discovery.

Journeying this path
is extremely radical.
It requires the transformation
of my vision.
It changes what I once viewed
as unsatisfactory
into an experience
of Wisdom.

This path
is criticized by religious people
because it requires
the death of Ego
which like institutional religionists
strives to dominate, control, and achieve.

This path
on which I wish to embark
is a gentle path,
but not one for weaklings,
indeed one for warriors.

I seek to be that warrior,
holistic in vision,
determined to accept reality, as it is,
with an uncompromising commitment to
Truth,
having the courage
to simply Be.

As a gentle warrior,
I admit my personal limitations,
with my gentleness
a sign of Strength.

I vow an unwavering commitment
to be gentle in order to be tough
and tough in order to be gentle.

Despite the scorn and derision
of the religionists,
this Path I do seek.

The Travesty

Many religious people
have made a travesty of Faith
by making it their biggest
Attachment.

By clutching man-made
doctrines, creeds, codes of conduct and
scriptural interpretations,
they clothe their faith in armor.

A sign of this kind of faith
is its militant stance.

For me, True Faith is gentle and loving.

A false faith tends to be
stubborn, inflexible, paranoid,
exhibiting a desperate need
to be right.

False faith, paranoia in disguise,
often turns violent,
with many religious fanatics
deeply insecure.

They feel a need to hold on to
some symbol of power
for their own peace of mind.

The symbol can be
an historical person, set of sacred writings,
religious doctrines, creeds, rites, and rituals.
Because their need to be right is so strong,
they attack whatever or whoever
undermines the power symbol,
with their faith imprisoning
rather than liberating them,
barricading instead of opening up,
indoctrinating rather than enlightening.

For me,
Faith does not mean
living a protected, fortified life.
The Faith Journey
exposes me
to all that Creation has to offer.

And Everything Belongs.

Jesus, so gentle and Loving,
was severe with the Pharisees of His time,
not because they were hypocrites,
not because they refused to accept Him,
but because of their
Idolatry.

The Pharisees idolized the scriptures
and their laws.
Jesus tried to free the Pharisees of His Time
and the hierarchists of our time
from their frozen state of rigidity
by pointing to a Living Truth,
(instantaneous and situational.
Truth
cannot be frozen
in thoughts, words, concepts, creeds, rites,
and rituals.

The Living Truth,
proclaimed by Jesus,
cannot be grasped or attached or co-opted,

It Must be Lived.

At Hand

For me,
being Born Again simply means
having a Spiritual Awakening.

For Jesus,
Baptism is not a religious ceremony
but a spontaneous event,
not controllable or predictable;
it blows where it wills
and you hear the sound of it,
but you do not know from whence it comes,
or whither it goes.

Jesus' vision of the Kingdom of God
is not some future place or external event
but a Way of Seeing
the here and now.
He says specifically that
the Kingdom of God
is NOT coming with signs to see
but that it is in our midst.

Hierarchists teach the Kingdom
as some future reward
to be earned by doing what they tell us.

For Jesus,
the Kingdom of God
is the Present Reality
breaking tradition with the Old Testament.

The old tradition
and the tradition embraced even now
by fundamentalist Christians
is that it is something for which
we must wait,
despite Jesus saying
"Look, it has already arrived;
It is at hand!"

The dualistic view
embraced by many religionists
is that the present world
and the Kingdom of God
are separate.
Jesus' one-world holistic view
is that this world
IS the Kingdom.
The ability to have this holistic view
is truly a Gift of the Spirit.
Unless one is born of water
AND the Spirit,
one cannot enter (see) the Kingdom.

Jesus taught that
the Spirit and Truth
always come together,
and we can thus
think of the Holy Spirit
as the personification of Wisdom,
interestingly
called SHE in Scripture....Sophia.

Seeing the Kingdom of God
At Hand
is what makes me whole.

Trying to escape the Present
or ignore it in anticipation of
some future reward
dis-integrates me.

The Kingdom of God
is truly
The Precious Present.

Love: The Path to Contemplation

The blind stirrings of Love in my life
are being fanned into a bright flame,
a raging inferno,
tending to be a factor
in all my decisions.

It has been stirring me
softly and sweetly
with a certain inevitability
against which
it seems useless for me to struggle.

I seem in the grip of something
more powerful than I,
that constantly tugs at my heart.

I am losing fidelity to rules and law,
in submission to
the guidance that Love provides.

Is this Love
that possesses me
the gateway to true Wisdom?

Like a burning candle,
it has enlightened, not only all around me,
but myself as well,
enabling me to see both my failings
and my God-given gifts and beauty.

I trust that, as John writes in his First Letter,
"God is Love
and when I Live in Love,
I live in God
and God in me."

Life Flows

Authorities in my past
gave me views
about things that happened in the past.
For a long time,
I kept those views frozen
as my own views.

I thought the *authorities* had it right.

And so, I was encased in ice.
My projections of the future
were mired in the frozen views of the past.

But Life, True Life,
is not ice-bound;
Life Flows.

Truth is always In Movement.

But the key is
the Quality of Mind and Heart
that I bring to the Present Moment.

I discovered that I must bring
to every single precious present moment
Joy, Compassion, and Equanimity.

What I bring to the flowing present moment
is what brings balance to life
and makes that moment beautiful.

I discovered that I must approach
each present moment
with a Precision of Presence
which, without gentleness and tenderness,
could become cutting or wounding.

My Life has been a flowing river
since Beauty came,
in my ability to see things
as they are
in the moment
and taking Joy in that,
even though
the moment flows
and constantly changes.

Those who wanted me to freeze my ideas,
those who wanted their ideas to be my ideas,
based their lives on exclusivity.

But I discovered that True Wisdom
comes in Inclusivity,
in being Open to All
that the river of life brings me.

I cannot be completely inclusive
unless I inhabit the present Moment
and
I cannot inhabit the present moment
if I exclude anyone or anything.
I cannot be completely inclusive
unless I fully inhabit the present Moment
and
I cannot inhabit the present moment
if I am exclusive.

I cannot be completely inclusive
unless I inhabit the present Moment
and
I cannot inhabit the present moment
if my ideas are the frozen ideas
given me by someone in my past.

Growth

I'd become too analytical,
too focused on the rules,
trying to *Do Good and Avoid Evil.*

I discovered that a true Mystic
is one who enters the Mystery
of God
As LOVE.

Life in Christ
is, after all, Mystery.
It is the Mystery that
the incredible Love of God
is the source of
who I am.

I had to move
from head to Heart
to see the world in its true reality.
God is hidden
in the everyday, ordinary reality.

I tended to treat creation
as a sort of backdrop to my life,
eventually realizing that
*every aspect of the cosmos
is Word Incarnate.*

I began to see that
Everything bears
the Infinite Love of God.

I realized that
Nothing earthly does not have
some Divine Dignity to it.

And I am part of God's Cosmic Family.

I know now that
everything bears its own unique distinct way
of reflecting God's Love.

My path to seeing this broader vision
was not through the recitation of rote prayers,
but praying instead to know
My true Self,
the Divine Within.

My path to seeing this broader vision
was the realization that
I was capable of emulating Jesus,
being as Compassionate, Merciful, and
Forgiving
as was He.

My path
was realizing that salvation is really only
Being Made Whole.
Being "Saved"
simply means
Responding to and Accepting
God's LOVE
in my life.
And I discovered that
when I can become Whole,
I can help Others become whole
as well.

One of the resultant joys
is that every encounter with an Other
is an encounter with the Divine.

I have had to lighten up and
Enjoy the Ride;
It's a Great Adventure,

An Adventure in Love.

A Moral Sexuality (Some Possible Criteria)

Love must be based on
a foundation of one standard of Justice for all,
Male and Female, Married and Single,
Hetero and Homosexual,
Young and Old.
Without a solid foundation of Justice for all,
Love becomes perverted.

The physical expression of love
between two people
should be based on the level of
Loving Commitment in the Relationship.

Sexual expressions of Love
should be evaluated based on
the motivations, intentions, and
consequences
of the acts shaped by Love.

Sexual expressions
should be motivated by Love.

The intentions of sexual expression
should be engagement of the whole person,
mind, body, feelings,
aimed at fulfillment
and Communion.

The sexual acts themselves must not be
loveless, coercive, debasing, impersonal.

A sign of true love
is a willingness to be responsible for the results
of sexual expression
including responding to each partner's need
for
continued nurturing and growth.

Love

Love involves commitment,
my commitment to the Other.

Love displays a willingness to risk,
to entrust myself to the Other.

Love expresses a Desire to Give
and to Open myself in personal nakedness
to my Beloved.

Love Desires to Receive,
whatever the Other will give of self.

Love is expectant,
recognizing the inexhaustible possibilities in my
Beloved,
anticipating that enriching novelty and
surprise
will emerge from the relationship.

Love respects individual identity.

Love is Communion,
my intimate relationship with Life,
a Sacramental Channel to the Divine.

Love is self-liberating,
allowing expression of my own authentic self,
releasing great potential for growth.

Love enriches the Beloved,
the result of my concern and care.

Love is Honest,
expressing truthfully and candidly
the meaning of our relationship.

Love is Faithful,
expressing the Uniqueness of the relationship
without possessiveness.

Love is Joyous,
exuberant in my appreciation of
Life's Gift
and Love's Mystery.

Feelings

Feelings are my bodily responses
animated by my intelligence and by my
spirituality.
Feelings are neither anti-rational,
nor irrational.
My feelings represent the wholeness
of my response
to my experiences.
My feeling response to reality
involves both my mind and my emotions.
My feelings are my response to
my experiences
with my total self.
Feelings are my ability to be deeply aroused
by what I experience.

Desire

The Hebrews used the verb *To Know*
as a synonym for sexual intercourse.
The sexual act at its best
is the union of desiring and knowing.

When I desire another
without wanting to have deep knowledge
of her,
without wanting to be in deep Communion
with her,
I am treating her as an object,
a means of self gratification.
it is in desiring and knowing her
that my partner is treated as self,
as treasured participant
in Communion.
To Know and to Desire
are parts of one act.

Communion

Communion does not mean absorption.
When my body-self is united with a Beloved
Partner,
we are emotionally and spiritually
intertwined.
It is an experience of Unity,
but not unification.
Each self respects the other's identity.
As God is the go-between of self and self,
the act is Communion with God
nurturing all human experience.

In a true sexual relationship with my partner,
I do not possess her,
nor in my relationship with God,
do I possess God.
But True Knowledge is Communion.
In my intercourse with a partner
or with God,
it is matter of participation, not possession.

Incarnation

My body is an instrument of Communion.
My body is language.
As such, my body is not merely my physical
substructure,
but indeed *Word* itself.
We as Christians recognize it in Jesus,
Word made flesh.
But, not just Jesus.
My body is the body-word of Love.

My Faith is an Incarnational Faith,
**a Faith in the repeatable and continuing
Incarnation of God.**
God is known to me
through human presence
Divinely embodied presence.
Body language
is the essential material of Christian Theology.

178

My sexual body as Word
is basic to my capacity
to experience and know God.

Hence

My sexuality
cannot adequately be considered merely
a sub-theme of moral theology or ethics.
The acts and relationships
which constitute the material of theology itself
are inescapably intertwined with my sexuality,
both in my sin and in my virtue,
in my relationships and my alienations and
separations,
in my wholeness
and in
my resurrection.

Meeting Past and Future NOW

Having spent too little of my conscious and
unconscious time
in the Present Moment,
I now strive to do that.

I am influenced by my past,
but am also influenced by my future
through anticipation
about what might happen then,
along with any related fear and anxiety.

So, though I know that the Future
does not yet exist,
my thoughts about it affect me
in the NOW.

The Past and the Future
do flow together for me
in the Whirlpool that is the Present Moment.

I carry in me the legacy
of what I did, felt, thought in the past.
My anticipations, fears, anxieties
about the future
strongly affect me NOW.

I seek to dispel these thoughts
by continuously telling myself that,
just as any feelings I now have about events
in the past
will not change the past,
fears and anxieties about the future
will not change the future.

So maybe now I can approach both my Past
and my Future
with an openness, an inclusiveness,
an acceptance,
by simply taking more time having

a long loving look at what IS.

Wisdom

How do I attain Wisdom?

Rigid beliefs seem the opposite of Wisdom.

Wisdom tolerates Mystery;
Wisdom requires Attention;
Wisdom is content without conclusions
or set explanations.
Wisdom embraces the Whole,
holding together things that appear
contradictory.
Beliefs seem the antithesis of Wisdom.

Myths and Metaphor
seem to be the very stuff of Wisdom.
My ego blocks Wisdom.
As long as I am centered in my own
sense of identity
I exclude opportunity for Wisdom.

Wisdom seems un-natural,
non-linear, non-conceptual, non-judgmental.
Wisdom encompasses all views,
all approaches,
is based on
Integration without rejection,
a grand mosaic.

Oh, my beliefs, my views, my perspective
may give me a glimpse of Truth,
but taking them as the whole Truth
is folly.
To have any chance of attaining Wisdom,
I must give up needing
to be right.

Wisdom is a Process.

When I feel inspired,
something is reaching me
from Outside me,
a hint of Wisdom.

The real problem for me
is that
as long as I am looking for Wisdom,
I will never find it.
Any effort I have made to attain it
has blocked it,
for Wisdom does operate conceptually,
defying analysis.

Wisdom is simply
Intimacy with Experience
without reason or analysis.

It is experience
viewed from Wholeness,
not looking outward,
but seeking inwardly.

Avenues to Wisdom for me
have been
Beauty, Humor, Skepticism and Absurdity,
Dialogue, Music,
Compassion, and Love.

Another avenue I must learn
is Impartiality,
despised by all vested interests,
all hierarchies.

To come to True Self
requires my acknowledgement
that Wisdom is not one thing,
not a thing at all,
but a process,
a process of recognizing my own ignorance
and becoming aware of myself
as part of a Greater Whole,
while moving toward that Wholeness
and starting again
and again.

My Consciousness

is infused by my feelings and my thoughts.
They are the basis of my individuality.

But I face a conflict between
my two purposes in life:
Individuation and Achievement
on the one hand
and
Empathy and Oneness with All on the other.

Most of my life
ego ruled,
feeding an endless need for approval
and success,
filling my consciousness
and
overruling the purer intention
of developing Compassion
and
Universal Awareness.

I am now striving to free my consciousness
from its imprisonment by ego.

My selfish habits and concerns
must give way
to the discovery of
My True Self,
my Eternal Spirit.

I am now trying to strip away
all the layers of ego and conscience
which have separated me,
not only from others,
but also from my True Self,
and
from my Creator.

Separation from my Creator
and imprisonment by my ego
likely were necessary steps
in the creation of my own unique
consciousness.
But in the process
I became fractured by selfishness
and aspiration.

In whatever time I have left,
I vow to focus
less on my ego-centered needs
and
more on Compassion and Empathy
so that
I might become
more truly Aware
and
One with All
and
My Creator.

Misguided Me

I spent most of my life
trying to be Happy
or trying to do something
that made me Happy.

What I discovered,
Oh so late in life,
is that what really gives me JOY
is making OTHERS Happy.

I get great Joy
from giving others
totally unexpectedly
something they really need or want.
Joy!

I get great Joy
in helping Others
along Life's Journey
overcoming Life's losses
finding a path
to Spiritual Growth.

Jesus taught it,
but I missed it:
OTHERNESS.

Even though Happiness is fleeting
dependent on happenings,
it gives me great
JOY
even in just providing moments
of Happiness
for Others.

Living with D***h

Living with death on my doorstep
may sound morbid to some,
especially the young
or those who are in denial.

But it has some advantages.

It enables me to
appreciate each sunrise, each sunset, each
day,
each moment,

say *I Love You*
before it's too late

stop putting off
things I must do

say *Thank You* to those who have gifted me
including family
and God

Forgive those who have hurt me
as the hurt seems far less important
with D***h around the corner

Speak the Truth
I have been stuffing all these years

Treasure all the small things in life
I took for granted all along the way.

I'm not ready to invite or welcome D***h in,
but living with the knowledge
that it's only a life moment away
helps me appreciate
the nearly 39 million moments I've lived

and this ONE

called *Now.*

Balance

The struggle
to balance effort and effortlessness
--both of which are needed--
is difficult.

When I am tempted
towards self-righteousness
by fulfilling all the religious externals
prescribed by institutional religion,
all I end up doing
is reinforcing Spiritual pride.

When I am tempted
to escape reality with distractions,
all I end up doing
is wasting the Precious Present Moment.

Instead I strive
at each moment
to do what brings me back to my Center,
my True Self.

I constantly seek
that balance
between detachment and dedication
with burning passion.

The Contemplative Life and the Active Life
are not mutually exclusive;
I need both
as each flows from the other.

Dear God,
help me find that Balance.

To Peace

Institutionalized Religion has failed
to provide adequate enough inspiration
to prevent the destructive environment
in which we now dwell.

Religion as institutionalized
has lost fundamental contact
with the Sacred Feminine
with its Unity, Peace, Beauty, Love,
and Compassion
because it has discriminated against
and repressed women,
guardians of that knowledge.

I think we must take two courageous
related actions:
Return to the Mystical Revelation,
at the core of religion,
stripping away all the divisive fanatical
trappings,
and
Be open not only to the Revelations
of ALL mystical traditions
in a spirit of passionate and authentic
Dialogue
but also to the Wisdom of the Divine Feminine.

We need to let the Divine Feminine
Consciously and Completely
enter our core
so that Mother God
can heal, refine, purify, harmonize,
and embolden us.

The Divine Feminine has always been
Present to us,
but we have lacked a True Mysticism
in not being totally receptive to Her.
The Divine Feminine in the fullness of Her Glory
must be totally present to us
in order to serve Peace and Unity
in the world.

Without doing so,
religions will continue to be
part of the problem,
and not the solution to it.

There can be no peace among nations
until there is peace among religions.

Stop Looking for God

My Spiritual Journey
changed dramatically
when
I stopped looking for God.

I had been acting as if
God were hiding out,
almost impossible to find,
either beyond the cosmos
or deep within me.

My Spiritual Journey
changed dramatically
when I realized that
God was looking for me,
the True me,
and
I needed to come out from hiding.

When I began to picture myself
through God's eyes
at my lost or hidden Self,
I discovered the Divine Joy
at my Awakening,
my True Self coming out of hiding.

My life became less anguished,
more trusting,
when I simply let God see
my True Self bloom.
I sensed a Divine Smile
as I no longer hid my self
from the True Love of my Creator.

My Spiritual Journey
changed dramatically
when I realized
I AM Worth looking for.

Accept

I barely know how to begin to value this life.
After all these years, I am still searching!
Even when I've had a piercing insight
or moment of Grace,
I don't know what to do with it
other than share it.

I generally measured my life
in terms of my needs
and desires.
I rarely remembered to say *thank you*
for my restlessness,
the dark valleys and stretches of
meaninglessness
that gave way to light.

Instead of some list of resolutions,
I will spend some time reflecting on
and accepting the whole of my life,
just as I am accepted by a force
or intelligence
greater than myself.

Enlightenment is not separate from the
movement to
a state of acceptance.

To understand is to accept,
and to accept is to truly love.

I found Grace in restlessness.
It struck when I walked
through the dark valley
of unknowing.
It struck when I felt separation,
deeper than usual.

I found it when my dissatisfaction with self,
my indifference, my weakness,
my hostility towards abusive church leaders
had become a real burden to me.

I looked for Grace
when the longed-for perfection of life
did not appear,
when my old compulsions reigned within me,
when my anger with institutional church
overran joy.

At times, a wave of light broke through
the darkness,
as though a voice were saying,

John, *You Are Accepted*.

199

I know now I am accepted,
not by religious fundamentalists,
but by my Creator,
accepted by that which is greater than me,
the name of which I do not know.
I do not ask for the name now
as I did of my Angel, Michael.
Perhaps I will find it later.

The Voice said,
Do not seek for anything;
do not perform anything;
do not intend anything.
Simply accept the fact that you are
accepted.

This is an experience of Grace.

I may not be better than before
and I may not believe more than before.

But everything is transformed.

Grace conquers sin
and reconciliation bridges the gulf of
estrangement.

Nothing seems demanded of this experience,
no religious or moral or intellectual imperative
or action-plan,
nothing but acceptance,

acceptance of the fact that

I am accepted

and to accept
is
to Truly Love.

Abandon Ship!?

Though I might feel safer

and more comfortable

simply residing on the Barque of Peter

(The Holy Roman Catholic Church),

I, like Peter,

must answer the call

to leave that comfort

and false sense of security

to

test my Faith

in/on

the Waters of Life.

(Without a lifejacket or being tethered)

My Commitment to Institutional Church

is less than total,
not because I do not appreciate the gifts
it has provided me along life's journey.

I see Institutional Church as less than sufficient
for me
because I have learned about
its limitations and shortcomings,
albeit with gratitude
for the graces it has brought me.

It is less than enough
because I have grown in my Faith
and have become more confident
about God
and about the Holy Spirit Within.
Is this not what Jesus taught?

I seek support, verification, validation,
and wisdom
not only from Church administrators,
the so-called Magisterium,
but from the people of God;

not only from official Teachings of the Church,
but from the Holy Spirit Within
and from my own human experience.

I have found new ways of being Church
with a Church Council, Vatican II,
clearing a path
and urging me to walk it.

I have surrendered former child-like patterns
of being Church
in order to reclaim gifts
gained by Baptism
and through Human Experience.

I must live out my life in the Love
preached and practiced by Jesus
in my own Good Conscience.

What is My Christian Destiny

There are no consciences walking around;
there are only human persons.
My conscience is I.
We are all human persons with a conscience.

How do I obey my conscience?
With two adverbs: intelligently and absolutely.
Intelligently means to inquire;
Absolutely means to obey without reservation.

But then how do I obey authorities
in the community?
Obey, yes, but guardedly and prudently.

But Freedom is an absolute condition
for a community,
meant for persons in the community to
blossom out.
Freedom is a divine quality.
God is free
and freely brings this universe into existence
and God's creatures cannot blossom out
unless they have freedom.

What is my Christian destiny?

To be a redeemer
like the Son of Man, Son of God, was a
redeemer.

Church

We live in a Church that is,
at this point of history,
full of turbulence.
Think of mountain rapids
that break into the quiet flow of a mighty river
on the lowland.
The waters meet, and there is turbulence.
This is what happened to the Church
at Vatican Council II.

There was a seemingly quiet flow
in the life of the Church
and then, the rapid came from the mountain,
so strong that it tended to divert the flow,
but also with its clean waters, giving new life
to the old river
and of course, turbulence.

Basically, the Council tried to modify,
even reverse
a quiet flow of the last thousand years,
beginning in the 11th century,
towards increasing centralization
in the western Christian community,
giving a lesser and lesser role to the people at
large.

That is what the Council tried to reverse
and of course there was/is resistance.

After every single major council in history,
there have been adverse reactions,
often lasting for a long time,
for a long time, one century, two centuries;
there seems no escape from that.

We have complaints,
and these complaints abound,
that the creativity and exhilaration
that marked the Council
and its immediate aftermath
are lost or are truncated.

Remember the great merriment
after the Council?

Now, a sort of gloom is descending
on the Church,
and it is very difficult for the community to
prosper
in gloom.
If gloom descends on a family,
then happiness in that family is indeed
destroyed.

Also there are complaints that the collective
wisdom and prudence of the people
affirmed strongly
in several conciliar documents,
principally in the Dogmatic Constitution
on the Church,
are not sufficiently honored.
There is little or no collegiality.

Sexual and Financial abuse in the Church
reveal deep internal problems.
The very fact that this happened
on a relatively large scale
speaks of problems of the heart, of the mind,
of the spirit
and the internal problems are both substantial
and also procedural.

But Jesus Christ is with his Church
every single day,
not just with the Church standing by,
but as an integral part of the body
in the sense that we are all members.

Jesus is there,
and we are organically connected
with Him in a mysterious way
that no words can ever explain.
Through our faith we know also
that God is sending the Holy Spirit,
the Comforter,
no less today than on
the day of the first Pentecost.
The Spirit is being poured out today.

We are snared
between troublesome humanity
in the Church and
the immense peace of God
in the same Church.

How can we make sense of all that?

We are caught up in an immense,
cosmic Divine Comedy,
a divine drama that is happening
on planet earth.

In this paradox of the hierarchical Church
and We as Church,
somehow, the mind of God is revealed to us.

We are baffled;
we are wondering what is going on.
Is it not true that
all this must have been in God's plan?

We are caught in the middle of this plan
and asked to enter into this play,
partly by accepting it fully,
the hierarchical Church
and We as Church;
partly, to take up a role in it.
And this role
can be even very uncomfortable,
uncomfortable because
I do not know what to do.

We are put on the spot and told,
"Now watch the play,
and then enter into it in a creative way."

The hierarchical Church is true.
"We as Church" is true.
That we are caught in this divine play,
this Divine Comedy, is true,
and that we are invited to enter into it
and there is no escape.
That, in a way,
is when conscience enters into it all.

How can I fulfill my own destiny intelligently
and responsibly
within a paradoxical, mysterious assembly
that I am told is my inheritance?

This assembly, which is one and divided,
the Church of Christ, which is holy indeed
but wounded by sin;
is an assembly founded
for the universal humanity,
yet at times before my own eyes
narrowly sexclusive and exclusive;
also an assembly rooted in the simplicity
of the apostolic college
and yet today burdened with heavy layers
of historical additions and secretions.
Within this assembly I am organically united to
Jesus and animated by this Spirit.

So how am I to fulfill my Christian destiny?
That's the question.

Conscience

God made man and woman to God's image.
What does it mean?
One of the Jewish translations says,
"God made human beings His own replicas."
God made human beings replicas of Godself,
not an image that is copied
from something else,
no little gods,
but the same sort, the same nature.
And that's how God created us.
Man and Woman God created us;
that is, God created us
endowed with intelligence,
the capacity to know,
and also with free will,
the capacity to reach out for
what is good.

And indeed we human beings,
these replicas of God,
have these divine sparks in ourselves.

We can grow into maturity
through progressing in knowledge,
and through steadily enriching ourselves
by reaching out for good things,
for what is valuable to us.

And we human beings cannot be perfected
to grow and flourish in any other way
than from inside.

As plants grow from the inside,
of course we can water them,
and they need sun,
and all that,
but ultimately they grow from the inside.
We human beings too,
ultimately grow from the inside
which means through our intelligence,
and through our conscience.
That's why conscience
is right at the heart
of human existence.

Our intelligence, in a way, is not free
because we must surrender to the truth.
Truth is revealed to us, but here is the mystery:
our will is free; it is God-like;
it can create or not create.

213

It can respond to the invitational something
that is good,
and it also can turn down such an invitation
by failing to act,
or by deviating from what is authentic
and really good.

Now God has given a living guide to help us
small creatures,
and that is conscience,
to direct us in finding, reaching for,
and appropriating what is good.

But to be free we can move or not move.
Freedom is a divine quality.

Outside of human beings in our universe,
no other living creature possesses it.

Before a decision and action,
the conscience guides,
and after each decision,
the conscience judges.
The conscience is always the ultimate judge,
to do or not to do.

Conscience judges all personal intents
and actions.
They all are subject to
the judgment of conscience;
but the conscience is I.
So again there is a paradox there.
I speak of the conscience
as I would speak of a third person,
and at the same time, it is I,
I talking to myself,
giving me guidance, instructions,
and even sitting in judgment over myself.

Even God respects this process.
God never forces anyone.
It's kind of frightening.

That's the dignity of human person,
that when God wants to touch me,
to talk to me,
God knocks on the door of my conscience.
"Will you let Me in?"
That is how faith is accepted.

God approaches every single person
through conscience;
but the guidance of the conscience,
and its judgment,
are not conceptual, or verbal,
or in propositions.

If we follow conscience, we are rewarded
with an internal peace and harmony.

Our whole being is involved in this process.
If we reject the guidance of conscience,
we are punished by internal restlessness.
That's the experience of all of us;
and this experience is reported
in the greatest pieces of world literature.

Authority of Conscience

What about the authority of conscience
versus obedience?
The authority of a person's conscience
is absolute.
Even God knocks on the door of the
conscience
and asks for admission.

St. Paul, the Apostle, realized that as well.

In Chapter 2 of his Epistle to the Romans
he says that God will judge the Jews
according to the Jewish law,
God will judge the pagans
according to the law
written in their hearts,
God will judge the Christians
according to the law of the Spirit,
who was given to them;
that is, according to whom they accepted
as a guide for their conscience.

God accepts the judgment, honest,
good judgment,
of conscience itself.

Shall we say our humble God who made
replicas of Godself,
and then keeps respecting them,
little replicas.
Conscience, in a way,
is a direct link to our maker.
It's a link to the Spirit of God.

For Christians it is now the Spirit of God
who humbly asks for acceptance
whenever God prompts a person to believe,
to hope and to love.

But conscience is not a lonely ghost;
it is an integral part of
the whole human person.

All the acts of conscience are,
and must be rooted in, generated by,
produced by, the whole person.
The person's sensitivity, accumulated
knowledge, critical intelligence,
all must contribute to the completeness,
to the perfection, to the authenticity,
of an act of conscience.

The act of the conscience
is the act of the whole person,
no less and no more.
The conscience of a lazy person,
who doesn't want to inquire about anything,
is a lazy conscience.

The conscience of an alert person,
curious, inquiring, looking for the best, is
precisely that--
the conscience of an alert person,
which means that we have the capacity
to perfect our own conscience.
It follows that a thorough, critical examination
of every project of conscience
is a requirement for a correct, and authentic,
and life-giving choice.

Whenever my projected action
concerns what is a value for a community,
I have the duty in conscience
to consider the community thoroughly;
but the advice I receive
need not be automatically accepted.
It should go also through the filter
of my conscience.

We know about prophets
who stood up
against the common values of a community;
and they were right.
They were touched by God;

and through them, somehow,
God was directing
not their own conscience only,
but the conscience of the whole community.

Blind conscience doesn't really make
good sense
because the children of God, blessed with
intelligence,
must not live in blind obedience.

Our conscience
is the conscience of an intelligent person.
To follow a blind guide
would be demeaning for a human person.

In every single act of conscience,
there is always a unique, personal,
intuitive element
that is not accessible to any other person
and the honesty of the one who is following
that personal intuitive vision
should be accepted and respected by all.

Authority in Community

Conscience is, obviously, internal
and obedience to conscience
is an internal act.

But we do receive orders,
commands as it were,
from the outside,
coming from some authority installed,
established by the community.

**All impositions by human authorities
must knock on the door of conscience;
All of them
are subject to be examined by critical
intelligence,
and by enlightened faith.**

Blind obedience is not fitting
for the general good.
I must cleanse my own mind
from false and distorted conceptions.

The customary legal monarchical
model of Church
is really not all that fitting
for a human community,
and certainly not all that fitting
for a Christian community.

The so-called laity
are not accidentally in the Church.
Clerics would look ridiculous with
out the laity.

When an authority overreaches
the mandate received,
it should be regarded as a breach
of fiduciary duty,
and the subject may correctly refuse to obey.

For this reason obedience to human authority
must always be guarded and prudent,
never absolute.
It cannot be absolute.

Freedom

Freedom is a condition for life in abundance.
It thrives in abundance.
I can live and vegetate without freedom,
but cannot be a full human person
without freedom.

Freedom in the Church is
also an absolute condition
for faith, hope and love,
no less than that.

What is freedom for the Church?
What happens when the Church
is given freedom?
There is exhilaration;
there is cheer and there is creativity.

There are more mistakes than before
- take that for granted –
but goodness is welling up;
and sooner or later,
the mistakes will be corrected.
That may be the reason why the Lord Himself
didn't give a Code of Cannon Law
to the disciples.

With Vatican Council II
we had an explosion of freedom
after a long, long era of deficiency
in that matter.
In the fall of 1962,
the assembled bishops discovered themselves
as endowed with freedom;
and their creativity suddenly welled up.
The Council gently swept away
quantities of the prepared material
that was put before them for approval,
and they created the documents, the
proclamations, that we possess.

Where did it come from?
Not from what was prepared.
It came out of their own creativity.
Why?
Because we had John XXIII,
who let them be free.

Vatican II liberated
the non-Catholic Christians
from condemnations.
Before the Council, they were heretics
and schismatics.

During the Council,
they turned into our brothers and sisters.
It was a liberation and there was no question
anymore whether
or not one could meet them;
one could participate in the same worship.

Vatican II finally and firmly
liberated the Church itself
from any subservience
to secular authority
when it affirmed and reaffirmed
religious freedom,
which was also a declaration for the Church
to be free.

It became like the humble Christ,
not going around among the nations
with power,
but in the more humble attitude of Christ
being there to serve.
It was a different Church.
The Church was liberated
because it was allowed, requested, ordered
to return to its own self.

There were mistakes
- of course there were –
how could you expect otherwise?
There were some aberrations.
How could you ever avoid that
among human beings?

And when there is no freedom, common
experience,
gloom descends on people.
And when there is freedom,
there is Joy.

Christian Destiny

What is my Christian Destiny?
What I should do?
How do I make sense of God's plan
in our world,
my place in the Church, as revealed.

This has double aspects: hierarchical
and We as Church.
I guess I must simply remember that I am
nothing, nothing, nothing else,
than goodness, goodness wanting to pour out
myself, Godself.
That is Love.

Do I understand the mind of God?
God allows people to disobey
so that mercy may shine.
God lets people sin abundantly,
because God wants to overwhelm us
with grace.

I step back and one cannot believe
anything else:
God is our God!

Now are we in a period
where Christians are allowed to disobey,
even disobey the Church Magisterium,
so that the immensity of God's love
can be revealed?

Am I thinking right?
Am I thinking wrong?
I am ready to be corrected.
But the question is there.
How can I deny the question?

I do not understand the mind of God.
I say it just like that.
My mind is enough only to raise some
questions.

So what is my Christian destiny?
Assuming that I have the gift of faith,
I know that I do not understand.
How could I with my little brain?

But I believe that whatever trouble there is
with hierarchical church is part of God's plan.

I believe God wants to reveal
Magnanimous Love
that has no other reason for being
than it is Divine.

So now, what is my Christian destiny?
I do not quite understand everything
and I do not pretend to understand it,
but what I understand is
**I am called to be a small replica
of this magnanimous God
and spread goodness all around me.**

Another Good comes into my mind:
Small is Beautiful.
What is that?

There are many people
who are expending immense energy,
trying to make reforms in faraway places
that they can never touch.
But they forget to be witnesses of
magnanimous love here and now.
Sometimes this need not mean more than
a cheerful "Good morning!"
What would happen if every Christian
dedicated himself or herself
to be a source of this magnanimous love
that reveals God's goodness,
no matter how hierarchical,
how wrong the Church may be.

Love is the Answer,
Whatever the Question.

Catholic Bill of Rights and Responsibilities.

1. Primacy of Conscience.

Every Catholic has the right and responsibility
to develop an informed conscience
and to act in accord with it.

2. Community.

Every Catholic has the right and responsibility
to participate in a Eucharistic community
and the right to responsible pastoral care.

3. Universal Ministry.

Every Catholic has the right and responsibility
to proclaim the Gospel and to respond to the
community's call to ministerial leadership.

4. Freedom of Expression.

Every Catholic has the right to freedom of
expression and the freedom to dissent.

5. Sacraments.

Every Catholic has the right and responsibility
to participate in the fullness of the liturgical
and sacramental life of the Church.

6. **Reputation.**
Every Catholic has the right to a good name
and to due process.

7. **Governance.**
Every Catholic and every Catholic community
has the right to a meaningful participation in
decision making,
including the selection of leaders.

8. **Participation.**
Every Catholic has the right and responsibility
to share in the interpretation of the Gospel
and Church tradition.

9. **Councils.**
Every Catholic has the right to convene and
speak in assemblies
where diverse voices can be heard.

10. **Social Justice.**
Every Catholic has the right and the
responsibility
to promote social justice in the world at large
as well as within the structures of the Church.

Our Ultimate Truth

The ultimate mystery of our being,
our ultimate truth,
is Love.
In us is an infinite desire
to give ourselves in Love.

Giving ourselves in Love,
losing ourselves
finding ourselves in Love,
with Love returned to us,
is the eternal pattern of the universe.

In the depth of our being,
we long for Love,
are drawn by Love,
to give ourselves in Love,
to surrender to our Lover.

This seems the very structure of our being,
built into our cells,
the deepest instinct of our souls.

Sin is the refusal to Love.
True Love is divine,
with all Love Holy.

What is This All About?

Though many have said
God's plan can't be known,
opening myself deeply to
the Spirit of Questioning
has become a truly motivating force in my life,
beyond the limits I'd ever imagined.

A Zen Master said
"The most important thing is
to find the most important thing."
For me,
the most important thing
has been living the Question,
Who Am I, really?

What is my totality,
right here and now,
both what I conceive outside me,
as well as what is inside?

For me,
the Spirit of Questioning
is a deep devotion to
the mysterious presence of life itself.
It is my longing for Wholeness,
to become one with my true Self.

My Questioning has resulted in a greater Faith.
Great Doubt; Great Faith.

Too long have I lived in the confines
of my thoughts.
In reality, thought has no power
over the all-pervading presence I am.
My thoughts only arise and dissolve
as more thoughts arise.

No matter what my mind recognized
as
what was happening around me,
actually happening was
an expression of Pure Presence,
where Truth is revealed.

I am becoming more and more aware of
how insubstantial thought is.
I always have the choice
to act upon my thought
or watch it dissipate.

If I keep my attention Within,
my desire for Truth
continually confronts me.

Is my True Self
my consciousness or my awareness?
They cannot be grasped
by my mind.
Though I get no answers to these Questions,
they help me realize
my actual Being in the world,
even though my mind is unable to understand
why this is so.

Am I separate from the Cosmos?
I ask myself,
Why is Questioning so important
when there is no answer.

There is no Why.

So I no longer try to find answers
to the Questioning,
but only attempt to stay with the reality of
Not Knowing,
staying with the Mystery.

I had assumed that
the Universe and I were separate;
My own self-inquiry, My Questioning,
challenges that assumption.

I believe
that dwelling in the Great Unknown of
Who Am I, really
leads to
the Great Awakening.
I just need to become the Question,
Who Am I, Really?

Truth is not found in concepts.
Reality is not an IT.
and cannot be grasped by my mind.
My role in life
is *not to know what reality is.*

I strive simply
to drink in each moment;
Here and Now.
The Present is the Source.
Here and Now
is one hundred percent identical
with every moment in the Universe.
When I Question this deeply,
I can awaken fully.

I am
What I Want;
I want
What I am.

The Climb

Climbing up
The Mountain of Life,
each of our paths is unique.

And each path takes many turns,
sometimes sideways,
sometimes even down
before heading up again.

Each path is fraught with hazards
and stumbling blocks.
Often I trip,
am stymied,
fall
and hang on for dear life.

I'm often tempted
to stop climbing
and build a little cabin or chateau
or
even set up a tent
just to rest and enjoy the view.
But I know
I cannot stop.
I must keep climbing.

Trouble is
I cannot see what's on top.
The Cloud of the Unknowing
keeps me from seeing my goal.

It takes Faith
and
Love
and courage
to pierce it.

Along the way,
I encounter many others,
each on his/her own path.
Sometimes our paths run parallel
and we help each other
as we stumble.
Sometimes our paths cross
and we share experiences and
provide guidance.

We help light each other's path.

As I encounter
and help others
on the way,
there seems a tendency
to want to hang on to them,
to bring them on my path,
or even take their path with them.

Sometimes the love I feel
from encountered travelers
drives me to want to merge our paths.

But I know
this cannot be.

Each path is unique.
Leaving mine for another's path
or
forcing another on my path
is
but a detour
in life.

Learning how to let go
is
a critical lesson I am learning
in climbing
The Mountain of Life.

Leaving behind the security
found in an other
is tough.
But I know
it is a false security.
I know that I must take my own path
through the Cloud of the Unknowing
to my ultimate destination.

And I know,
although each path is unique,
all paths lead to the same place,
to Love,
to God.

I know that
Letting Go
allows each of us
to find our way
so we CAN all be together again.

Spirituality

Spirituality is not solely
prayer and devotion
alongside my secular life.

Spirituality
refers to my entire life
as it is intentionally related to God.

My Spirituality
is the framework for
my believing life in the world.

My daily life
can no more be divorced from Spirituality
than my prayer from daily life.

Spirituality
is anchored in and validated by
the way I live.

My Spirituality
embraces and enjoys
my secular life.

The clergy live in the secular world
as much as I,
but their mission is to maintain
a worshipping community
where God's affirmation of the secular
is celebrated.

The clergy, thus,
are not so much set apart for sacred things,
as directed to a vitally important,
but *less central role*
in the mission of the church.

The primary characteristic of Spirituality
is
Freedom.

I was created,
as were ALL others,
to be unconditionally free in the world.

Being Free is common to All humans
and is fundamental to our Spirituality.

We are created
with intelligence
and capable of deep feelings,
aware of our world.

We have a dynamism toward questioning,
exploring, and understanding.

We have the capacity for
problem solving, system building,
knowledge, and Wisdom.

The world is ours
to maintain,
to improve,
to save.
The baseline for Spirituality
is the world.
The Spiritual Project
is the world.

We are taken up with the world,
fully engaged in the world,
interested in things of the world.

I can and do affirm the higher reality of God,
while trying to
live a life of integrity,
love,
build community,
and make the world a better place to be.

Though institutional religions
call us to rely on
external authorities,
hierarchy, scripture, etc.,
which are important sources of wisdom,
Freedom lies
in following the call of

The Holy Spirit

resident deep within each of us.

External authorities
only serve to trap us,

The Holy Spirit,

to Free us.

Satisfaction

There is nothing more boring
than listening to a satisfied person.
He spends so much time building walls
around what he says
that he says nothing at all.

People who say they are Satisfied
are too concerned about being acceptable.

I am not concerned about being acceptable.

My concern is yielding enough to the One
who possesses me from within
that He can do through me
whatever He wants to do.

Folks who are Satisfied
never change the world.
They never affect society.
They live safely within the boundaries
of the status quo,
never challenging the forces that control
society,
the culture,
or the church system.

They believe that by reinforcing what is,
they will encourage folks to move on.

Satisfaction is the bane of progress.
It leads us to believe everything is
as it should be,
when in reality we are desperate for change,
anxious to see and hear from the Lord
concerning the things still locked
in the heavens.

Though the heavens are pregnant
with God's purposes
and
eternity dips into time and space,
Satisfied folk explain away
the restlessness within.

Satisfied folk redirect our focus
to what has always been.
They have the uncanny ability
to make the hungry
feel guilty for their hunger
and
the restless feel rebellious for their questions.

Satisfied people
are what everybody likes
to have under their control.
Satisfied people don't ever rock the boat.

But the Reformation never would have
happened without dissatisfaction.
The Renaissance
never would have happened
without dissatisfaction.
The great revivals
never would have happened
without dissatisfaction.

Dissatisfaction is the key to our growth.
It questions what we have done,
why we are doing it,
and where we are going.

An Adventure Waiting to Happen

Satisfaction
tries to convince us
there is nothing new under the sun.

Everything is new under the sun.

Satisfied folk love to quote
a frustrated and depressed old man
who cries out in his depression,
"There is nothing new under the sun!"
But to our tiny masses of gray matter,
everything is absolutely new.

God may know everything,
but I sure don't.

For me,
every day is an adventure waiting to happen.
Every day is an irreplaceable opportunity
to see, hear, and do things
I have never even imagined could happen.

Each day holds the possibility
—no, the probability;
no, the certainty—
that the heavens will open above me and
His Presence will flow within me creating an
atmosphere of wonder and awe
that will most certainly change me
and the world around me.

To be sure, there is nothing new to the Lord,
but for us there are new mercies, new hopes,
new possibilities
opened to us every day
—if we are dissatisfied enough
to be open to them.

God Talks to Us Out of the Box

God always talks to us outside the box we
have constructed for ourselves.
You know that box.
It keeps you safe and assured
that you are fine
just as you are.

Our nature is to always define circumstances,
feelings, dreams, hopes, and possibilities
within the parameters of what has always
given us contentment.

This box assures us that we are, well, satisfied.

But this thought is not new.
Humans have always tried to re-box
what God has un-boxed.
Jesus warned us not to put new wine
into old wineskins.

Yes, the most boring person in the universe
is a satisfied person.

God Sounds Outrageous

God speaks to us outside of our paragons.
Everything He says to us sounds outrageous.
Our tendency is to dismiss those things
that are risky.
But when we dismiss the outrageous,
we too often dismiss God.

When God says something to us
that we have never heard before,
it often sounds exciting,
even though it may bring fear to our hearts.

Sometimes that fear turns to exhilaration
at the thought of doing something
so different.

Subconsciously, however,
we take a familiar course of action.
In our minds, we visit all the people
who are important to us
to determine how they will react
to this outrageous thing we have just heard.

Once the votes are cast,
most of the time we dismiss this outrageous,
albeit exhilarating, thing we have heard,
simply because most of the people we care
about
and who are important to us
dismiss it.

Even though we believe it,
even though it made our heart sing and burn
within us,
we reject it because our friends have too.

That is why so many end up doing
what has always been done.

Too many people fear the outrageous.
They fear anything that God says
outside the box
they have created for themselves,
which, by the way,
they have secretly learned to despise.

We all like to think of ourselves
as so open minded,
so charismatic, so Spirit-filled,
when in fact we have created a box in which
everything we believe is locked.

It keeps us satisfied.

Satisfied people never change the world.

They put you to sleep.

Satisfaction is not in the person.

Satisfaction is in the Body of Christ.

Grounded

I discovered me
in the thick, mucky area
where
reason, analysis, and resolution
don't have much effect,
a place
fundamentally irrational, enchanted,
bewitched,
sometimes the source of inspiration,
often the root of confusion.

I needed to be rational and analytical
to survive in the world,
but to connect with
my True Self, deep within,
I had to see through the façade of life
to my inner poetry.

As I began to live from
the ground of my being,
I was able to read the signs,
hints of what to do,
living close to the mysterious,
giving up my former need
to explain everything.

I now take my Intuitions
Seriously,
attentive to the mysteries around me,
acting from
the fog of insight
I draw from it.

Guidance often comes from
deep within.

In the process,
I discovered new riches
and
new sources of meaning.

Contrary to those who think
I'm no longer grounded
at risk of flying off into space,
I'm more deeply grounded,
than ever
Rooted deep within
to Mother Earth
and
Beyond.

Happiness or Joy

Happiness comes from the word 'happen'.

But the smiles and laughter of happiness
Only seem to come with

Good happenings,

Good Fortune, Success, Prosperity,
A Pleasant Experience, or
Exceptional Well-Being.

Happiness is a Feeling

Sharing times in my life with

Other feelings

Including Sadness.

Joy is not fleeting, not temporal.

Joy is founded in the Divine.

Joy is Long Term Contentment
Knowing I am Loved by God.

Joy sustains me through
Good and bad happenings.

Joy is a Calm deep within.

Joy thrives in Simplicity,
Gets lost in the clutter in my life.

Joy causes and is strengthened by
Not worrying what others think,
Not procrastinating,
Keeping my promises,
Not discriminating,
Not judging,
Focusing on the Good in others,
Giving up Negative attitudes.

In Joy,
I see Creation as Beautiful,
Life as a Gift.

Each day is Gift.
Each moment.

Joy enables me to
Live out my Life in Love
Bringing me Great Joy.

I Rejoice to the extent
I Love.

Joy is Profound
In times of Solitude and Silence.

Joy is
Giving up my plan for the Cosmos
In favor of God's Will.

With Love,
I can experience
All manner of happenings,
Good and Bad,
Bringing me
Great Joy.

True Love
Is occasioned by Joy
And
Brings Joy.

God as Love

Love does not suffer from
a lack of conditions,
but, in fact,
is reinforced by it.

Love gives itself.

The Gift of Love
does not require
acceptance of it
or a place to accommodate it
or a condition to assure
or confirm it.

God as Love
transgresses constraints.
No condition
can restrict Love's initiative,
amplitude,
and ecstasy.

Love loves without condition;
God loves without limit or restriction.

No refusal rebuffs or limits
God as Love,
requiring not the least consideration.

My impotence
is not enough to disqualify
Love's initiative
or accomplishment.

Love gives
of its giving
without restriction, reservation or mastery,
abandoning itself
exceeding the limits of its own gift,
transplanted outside itself.

The transference of Love
outside itself
without end or limit
prohibits need for a response.

God as Love
holds nothing back,
transcending itself
where nothing
can contain the excess of
absolute giving.

God as Love is gift
which gives forever.

Ministry OUTSIDE the Box;
LIFE Outside the BOX

Invited to speak at a Conference
with the Theme
"Ministry OUTSIDE the Box,"
I had to ask myself,
How/Why did I move
Outside the Box?

I never planned to move outside the Box.
I was essentially
a Pay-Pray-Obey Catholic
for over fifty years of my life.
All of my formal education
was in parochial institutions
(though the Jesuits at John Carroll University
might be considered resident on
the inner part of the outer edge).

All of my children were Baptized
inside the Box
and dragged to weekly Liturgy
as long as we could do so.

261

I thought I was content
inside the Box
paying my dues,
praying in the prescribed manner,
obeying the rules
to earn my
pass into heaven.

Thank God,
I was pushed, called, cajoled, forced
Outside the Box;
God was NOT resident in that Box!
What/Who pushed?

The Guys in control of the Box
had a swinging back door out.
They abused little children
and protected the abusers,
perpetuating the abuse.

The "celibate" Guys in control of the Box
were not so celibate.
The Pay part
of my pay, pray, obey,
was not being used for
the Good I thought it was;
much of it spent by and for
the box-controllers.

The Obey part
of my pay, pray, obey,
related to
rules which were
not only discriminatory,
not only man-made,
not only spiritually stifling,
but also,
Totally Un-Christlike.

The rules were created
to keep people
inside the box,
while keeping trouble-makers
outside the box.

Yes, God was not resident In a Box,
But neither was trouble-maker Jesus!

The Pray part
of my pay, pray, obey
pushed me out of the box
and at the same time
called and cajoled me out of it
as being rote, shallow, repetitive, dogmatic,
focused on formulas, superstitions, and beliefs.
I needed more;
My Spirit needed more;

Life was more;
Love was more.

People lived and died
in the box
never questioning their Faith,
never expanding their Faith.

Thanks Holy Spirit,
for blowing my spark of Spiritual Thirst
into a Raging Inferno,
for Seducing me
Outside the box.

After retirement from 32 years in Commerce,
I thought about
Ministry within the box,
joining the box-controllers
albeit only as a subservient Deacon.
Thanks, God,
for that not being a chosen path.

Instead, "I did it My Way"
Hospice Volunteer,
Master of Arts in Pastoral Ministries,
Certified Bereavement Counselor,
Free-Lance Author, Speaker, and Poet,
Spiritual Companion,
Trouble-Maker Rabble-Rouser,
Consoler of those Grieving Loss of Life
in the Box,
Helper of those needing to escape it,
Celebrant of the Good Life
Outside the Box.

I don't know if it was My Way
or the Way ordained for me,
but I'm sure Joy-Full
I found it
and am traveling it.

It seems that
the people to whom I Minister
are outside the box
or at least need to be;
those discriminated against
by the box-controllers,
(married men, women,
gays and lesbians, those divorced,
the alienated, and us trouble-makers)

265

and perhaps most importantly
those the Holy Spirit is helping to discover that
life inside the box
is not life at all,
but spiritual death,
or at best paralysis.

But,
Trouble-Maker Ministry Outside the Box
is not all peaches and cream;
Ask Jesus.

Friends and Family inside the box
separate themselves from me.
The Box-Controllers and their idolizers
deride and exclude me.
There is always a price to pay
and
It can be a lonely path.

But I think the Box may be crumbling;
so many are growing out of it
that it can't support all the Box-Controllers
sitting atop it.

The Flame of the Holy Spirit
seems to be casting a brightness into the box
exposing the swinging back doors
and the hidden nooks and crannies
maintained by the box-controllers
for all to see,
enabling many inside the box
to see that
a pay-pray-obey fully punched ticket
is good only for a life-time ride
on the merry-go-round
Inside the Box.

There are no two
Ministries Outside the Box
exactly alike, completely identical;
It's more simply like
using one's unique God-given Gifts
to help others
wherever the need.

Instead of pay-pray-obey,
I chose to follow the call of the Holy Spirit
(out of the comfort zone onto a Great
Adventure)
and to
Go, Grow, and Glow.

Send me no Gurus,
only Fellow

There's nothing worse,
nothing more boring
than being with people
whose minds are made up,
who know the answers
to life's burning Questions.

They either take your time
explaining why they are right
and/or
trying to convince you
to accept their answers
to life's unanswerable questions.
True Dialogue is not possible.

There's nothing more interesting,
nothing more exciting
than being with people who,
just like me,
are searching, seeking, questing
the meaning of life,
searching, seeking, questing
our purpose in being here,
some answers
to life's burning Questions.

We share experiences,
missteps along the way,
possible answers,
sorrows and joys along the way,
pebbles of Wisdom,
learning from
and **Listening** to each other.

True Dialogue.

I seek no Gurus, only loving friends
who will share their Journeys of Exploration
with me.

Finding Love; Finding God

<u>My True Self (and my Creator) Revealed in Action</u>

I am most truly myself
when I see, hear, think, judge, love, believe,
hope.
I access my self
when I act.

By being open to experience,
by searching for meaning,
by seeking truth,
by giving myself in Love,
by living in faith,
I find my true self
as a meaning-making self,
as a truth-seeking self,
as a self in Love.

I am always interacting with the Cosmos,
never apart.

My open, self-transcending self,
disclosed in the consciousness
of myself in action
is my first true inkling about my Creator.

God has meaning to me,
not as a puzzle to test me,
not as an idea that casts a positive light on all,
but as fulfillment of
the dynamic self
that I am.

A Self-Transcending Child of a Self-Giving God

My Self as a self-transcending self
looks for fulfillment
in life, meaning, value, relationship, and Love.

Inspired by the Sprit.
my self-transcending existence
is enabled
to break free of cosmic dread
and servitude,
to be Free
with the ultimate mystery of reality
in a nurturing self-giving Love.

The energy of
my Creator's own Love
has been poured into my heart
through the Holy Spirit.

271

The self-transcendence I seek
in asking, seeking, knocking at the door,
is fulfilled in
the Self-Giving Love by God.

My own self-transcendence
is truly a connection
to the Creator,
the Triune God.

Being Human is Questing

To be human
in a self-transcending mode
means that I must live within
an horizon of limitless mystery.

Even as the mystery attracts me,
I must resist the effort
to possess it or
to comprehend it.

Through human consciousness,
the universe becomes
aware of itself
as meaningful,
a limitless realm
of intelligibility.

My questions can be answered,
only serving to raise more questions.
Explanations can be given,
only raising more questions.

The universe appears to be
just one big Question,
*What is the meaning
of all that has been found meaningful?*

My Existence in Divine Love

The fulfillment of my existence
is akin to
a transcendent
Being-in-Love.

How does that relate to the Divine?
God is the Original Lover,
loving without the need for human merit.
As a child of God,
the gift of Love has been infused in me,
as mystery.

God's Love is manifest in creation
as Divine Self-Involvement,
Self-Uttering Word.

I have become conscious of it
through recognition and affirmation
of
my worth.
The Word became flesh.
My self-transcending self
unfolds in the presence of
the Self-Giving God.

True Love, Divine Love, is Unconditional,
even to the point of crucifixion,
ultimate Self-Giving.
I Respond to such Love
in my own self-giving.

Love cannot be not defeated.
Living in the Energy of
Transformative Love,
I can experience
a Peace nothing else can give,
a Joy no one can take away.
it is a Love
nothing can diminish,
a Life Beyond Death.

Love is communicative,
inspiring Faith, Hope, and Love
in Truth.

The Gift of Love
forms the Body of Christ,
True Church,
the People of God.
When I collaborate with Divine Love,
I am in Communion
with all of Church.

The Unconditional Divine Self-Giving
looks to
a new heaven and earth,
a new creation,
when all shall be one,
when God will be everything to everyone,
the Kingdom of God,
my hope for
the Ultimate Vision of God.

Being In Love

I can only make my way
through my passion for human existence
to self-realization
through self-transcendence
by seeking
Meaning,
Truth,

by seeking
Value,
Beauty,
Sacredness,
and
Love.

This self-transcendence
is not a journey into the meaningless,
or the imaginary,
or something
unwise, untrue, or unreal.
It is to be in a state of
Being-in-Love.

When I am in
an authentic state of Being-in-Love,
I sense the True Worth of
the object of my Love.

When I am
a Being-in-Love,
I seem ever disposed
to reach beyond myself
into the Other's world of experience,
manifesting itself in
compassion and collaboration.

With the Divine,
it is not that God has Love,
but that
God is Love.
God is unrestricted pure
Being-in-Love.
God as Being-in-Love
is fully conscious,
a state of utter
self-transcendence,
an infinite affirmation
of the worth of such Love,
an unrestricted commitment
to being Love
in every conceivable instance.

The Divine Being-in-Love
implies a three-fold subjectivity:
The Creator as the Originating Lover,
The Savior as the Self-Expression of that Love,
The Spirit as the Inexhaustible
Loving in Action.

God is
infinite self-realization in Love,
where Love and Self-Transcendence
are utterly identified.
Whereas I have to reach and expand
in order to achieve
Being-in-Love,
God is totally in that state.
The Divine Mystery
is an eternally self-constituting activity
of
Being-in-Love,
One Divine Consciousness
articulated as Trinity.

It is Love
without origin,
uttering itself in Truthful self-expression,
always True to itself in Self-Giving.

The Mystery of God as Love

God as Love
is Mystery
communicated by analogy
with what I find
in myself.

I am my best self
when
I am Being-in-Love,
when I am most self-transcending
to what is Good and Loveable
as with God.

But God does not simply *have it;*
God is this Love
in utter transcendence
in the self-expressive Word,
and the unrestricted Self-Giving
of the Spirit.

The Love
that God eternally is,
keeps on being Love.

The Divine Self-Communication
and my human self-transcendence
meet
in the context of the Mystery of Love.

In my experience of the reality
of the Self-Giving God,
the Love that
brings me into being
is revealed.

The Triune God of Love

God occurs in my experience
as Mystery
of
Love,
an original
self-giving Love,
establishing its own Truth
and
meaning in the Word,
endlessly creative
in the abiding Spirit.
God is Mystery
of
Being-in-Love.

This Self-Giving Love
presupposes
a Self in the Giver,
a Self in the Gift,
a Self in the Giving,
the Trinity.

The Mystery of this Triune God
is the revelation of
Love's Source,
Love's Meaning,
Love's Transforming Power.

Climbing To the Peak

A lifetime seeking Truth
(climbing the mountain of life)
has led me to

I AM
because
LOVE IS

at this moment
(on this plateau.)

This five-word statement
seems to embody my reality,
my being,
in relationship with the Divine,
My Truth.

But what is Truth?

Is it something out there,
something to be discovered or perceived?
Jesus said he came to bear witness to it.
He said He was the Way, the Truth, the Life.

Is Truth *Being?*

Plato said Truth is the memory
of who we are and what we know
from all eternity.

In Sanskrit,
Truth is *that which is.*

If Truth is Reality, Pure Reality,
is it one?

Is my

**I AM
because
LOVE IS**

the one truth for all?

Truth
must be infinite,
unlimited,
and with an infinite number of facets.

Each facet of Truth
must be *True*
without encompassing
all of Truth
which is infinite.

I believe each path
up the Mountain of Life
is unique
even though we are all headed to
the same peak.

With each path unique,
the view from the mountain is unique
depending on the eyes of the beholder
and the slope of the mountain
at a particular moment.

Truth may be One,
but apprehended and represented
uniquely and distinctly by each and every
climber's consciousness and position on the
Mountain.

The View through my eyes
and heart
at this juncture on my climb
is

I AM
because
LOVE IS.

I will only be able to see
the All-Encompassing View of Truth
when I reach the Peak.

We can then share it together.

About My Dying

I want my dying
not to be experienced as a dark and
depressing time.

I wish my dying to be a natural culmination
of a long and complete life.
I do not see Death as a defeat,
nor an obliteration of my being,
but as a transition to something even greater.

I hope I can welcome death.

I hope the end of my life will be
special time of sharing
filled with an intimate, intense immediacy
unlike any other care setting.

I want to face dying as I approached life;
with Love.

Dying is not separate from my life,
but is a continuation
of all that has come before;
it is the last part of living out my life.

I choose NOT to hide death and dying away
behind the cold, hard walls
of a hospital corridor
where "others" can provide care;
No Way!

I know that some friends and family
may want to hide from their own fears
and the painful experiences
they might encounter
were they to be present
during the dying process.

A fear of death
by those around me
could isolate me
if they wish to continue as normal a life
as is possible
under the circumstances.

While some may wish to hide death away
from sight,
I want to die at home
surrounded by those I love.
For me that is good end-of-life care.

286

Whatever you do, don't put me in a facility.

I wish the period of my death
to be not only a time for loss,
but also a time for sharing, communicating,
serving
and experiencing.

I have watched
the "sands of time" move inexorably
through the hour glass,
demanding that I take note
of increasingly prominent signs of my aging:
gray hair, changing shapes, wrinkles,
weakness,
pain or disease.

If I allow myself to be objective,
I see that
many around me
are stricken with accidental injuries, sickness
or death each year.
I inevitably suffer
and am succumbing to old age
and death.

Rather than being a material accident
without meaning,
I view life as a gift.
I view life as a spiritual journey
with lessons to learn through every challenge.

All of life--including my dying--becomes
meaningful.

A lack of appreciation for the miracle of life
would lead me to find fault with death itself
or the suffering that is part and parcel
of this world.
It is very common to try and fix blame
for the losses that occur in our lives.

I trust my loved ones will not forget me,
but that they continue to move on with life
and do whatever they can
to make this world
a better place.

In time, they will relinquish any preoccupation
with grief
and with the past.
They will never forget.
They will never lose the connection
with me.

Pain becomes unbearable
when we believe we are isolated,
unloved and alone.
I could be consumed by my own feelings
of fear, grief, guilt or anger.
I refuse to shut out friends and family
in my dying.
My Hospice doctors, nurses and others
who care for and serve me
know that one of the greatest achievements
they can have in the care setting
is to be there and "connect" with me,
to share in the moment,
to let me know I am loved and recognized,
to let me know that
I am positively appreciated,
to "reach" past the wall and touch my soul,
so that a mutual recognition is felt,
heart to heart.

We are all alone in a way,
but it is the loss of feeling "connected"
to others or God that hurts so much.
The betrayals, pains
and disappointments in life
make it even more difficult to trust others
or to trust the process of life itself.

The loneliness and depression that may arise
could eventually lead me to shut myself off
even more completely.

One of the paradoxes of life
is that in order to free myself from that
loneliness
and self-imposed isolation,
I must be again willing to trust and reach out
to others and God.
We all have a need to feel loved, and so do I,
especially in my dying.

Those who care for me
have the privilege of serving
and sharing their love.
Although many fear being around me dying,
I need those they care about
to visit and be with me.

I do not need casual visits from those
who are not involved.
While those witnessing me dying wonder what
to say or do,
there are no special words or phrases
that are going to magically
"make it all better."

My dying and death
are not something that can be "fixed."
It is something that must be acknowledged
and accepted.

The prospect of dying forces me to
contemplate
the meaning of life,
to review my actions in life,
to confront my ultimate aloneness.

Many are afraid and overcome with loneliness
in their despair,
but I will try to "take death on"
and let go of this life.

Not everyone experiences "aloneness"
as "loneliness."
I could spend days, weeks or even months
all alone
and never feel "lonely."

What makes the difference?

I am not "lonely".

I have been filled with a sense of purpose, a
focus,
a feeling of "connectedness"
that bars any feeling of loneliness from
entering me.
I know I belong.
I know I have a place in this world.

I know I have been/am loved.

I know I have a purpose in this life
and love to share.
I face death with this attitude
and hope to be at peace
when the end comes.
And the love I have for others
has made itself known
in a million ways.

I have tried to reach out to others,
encouraging, comforting, loving, helping,
sharing with them,
nurturing them till they are strong enough
to trust,
helping them to stand on their own in their
"aloneness"
and set out along their own paths.
They are no longer afraid.

I will try to comfort those around me in my
dying!

I perceive and accept my ultimate
"aloneness"
and my connectedness with others,
with all of life and the Creator of all life.
I am ready to experience the next step
and the world that awaits beyond.

I am not afraid.

The bitter pill that challenges me
can be swallowed.
My loving approach to life will not be broken
by the losses
or hurts I have experienced.

Though I may not be able
to immediately forgive
those who deeply disappointed me,

Though I may not be immediately able
to accept
the horrible injustices I witnessed,

Though I may not be immediately able to
surface
from the depths of my rage
when those I love were hurt and swept away,

Though I may not be immediately able
to embrace my pain
and transcend it,

there is a way to turn the poisonous depths of
despair into hope.

I focused on doing what little I could do
in my own world
to help others.
I opened my eyes and heart
to the needs of the others around me.

Their needs cried out to my heart:
choosing to care for them had the power
to heal me.

Being willing to accept the help of others
is not only humbling, but also healing.
In serving as well as in being served,
I am healed in some way!

Strange it is that while I feel so powerless
over the hardships of this life,
I had only to give of the little I had,
to find that I had so much more.

And the more I gave of myself,
the more I had.

The awareness of suffering's universality
became a raft
that helped me to make the journey
from isolation to connection,
from self-centeredness to concern for others,
from bitterness to gratefulness,
and from doubt to faith.

I reached out with real compassion,
a compassion that truly connected me
with the ones I served.

If I consider the wonders of the universe
and remember and focus on the kindnesses
that I have received,
I awaken within myself gratefulness
for whatever good fortune
I have had in my life.

Willingly accepting my reality,
including its pain,
I can move forward to truly live,
not by focusing on myself only,
but by realizing my purpose
and loving that which inspires me.

There are endless opportunities to serve,
none of them unworthy of pursuing.
For as long as there is life,
there is an opportunity to serve
and help others in some way or another.

Even my dying can serve,
help or bring healing to others around me,
this service given to my surviving family
and friends.
This is one of the reasons
that choosing to end the life
of even a dying person is wrong.

We all have pain in this life.
If I struggled to rid myself
of the suffering that must in some way
accompany this life,
I would find nothing but continued pain
and isolation:
a very bitter pill.

There is nothing wrong
with caregivers using all medical means to
relieve my physical pain.
We must do everything possible
to relieve pain.

But if I accept the suffering
that still comes my way
and appreciate the greatness of God's love
for me,
I am comforted.
My pain becomes bearable.

When I accept and willingly shoulder
the burden that is given to me in my life,
I find my burden lightened.

I am able to swallow
(what I thought would be) a bitter pill:
the simple reality of this truly beautiful life,
from birth through death.

Love, John

Sacred Relationship

I try to treat each encounter,
each relationship with an Other,
as a Sacred Meditation.

When I can,
a beautiful tenderness enters;
Care and Compassion
become part of the encounter.

When I can,
many of the mistakes I used to make,
aggression, skepticism, failure to listen,
disappear
because I am able to focus
on the *Essence* of the other.

And my opening up to them
brings up things in me
that need to be healed;
I gain a deeper sense of
my True Self
which brings a Joy and Delight
into the relationship.

A key for me
to spiritualizing my relationships
has been the recognition
that everyone
is a different facet
of
the Diamond that is God.

Spirit of Love

God becomes actively present to me
inviting me into intimate union
through Love.

Whenever I live in love with an other,
it is the Holy Spirit,
God as Love,
that is the Source.

When I love an other,
I become
a *Gifted Presence* of
God as Love
to that person
and that other person
Gifted Present to me.

We become *Present*
to each other
in the deeper and deeper recesses
of our True Selves.

We can share most intimate thoughts,
moving to *Communion*
with each other.

God becomes real
for me and the one I Love
in the expression of Love.

*Triune God
is indeed
Source of Love,
Love embodied,
Love enacted.*

God is . . .

God is the everlasting light
of awareness
in all, behind all, beyond all,
intimate to all,
encompassing everything.

This totality
is boundless Love
which thrives in its vitality
in the matrix
that is Trinity.

God is beyond human comprehension,
though we experience God
as we are able.

Though God is ungraspable, perfect, and free
of all limitations,
I experience the Divine
as God
Mothers me,
encourages me,
challenges me,
and consoles me.

God as Love
for me
is intimate and personal
given to me
in complete freedom.

God challenges me
to realize and actualize
who I truly am.

In God as Love,
I am
awakened to
Compassion, Sensitivity, and Love.

Moving with Honesty to Realization

I've been playing with light
thinking I was making Spiritual progress.

I've been exploiting mystical ideas
and experiences
for my own delight.

I did not realize
that the purpose of
all I have experienced and learned and
written
was to make me a servant
of Divine Love
in action in the world.

I did not realize that
Grace has indeed opened
Divine Realms for me
in order that
I can be devoted and humble enough
to dedicate
all my thoughts, emotions, actions, and
resources
to helping others
awaken to their own inner Divinity
and responsibility for *Sacred Action*.

I now feel the call
to jump into the furnace
of God as Love
that embraces all things,
to give the rest of my life
to spread and embody
the passion of
God as Love,
which lies within every human heart.

I know I must take up the challenge
and live in and spread
Divine Compassion,
God as Love.

The Ultimate Mystery

of being,
the Ultimate Truth
is
LOVE.

It is the essential structure of reality.

There is in my Being
an infinite desire
to give myself in Love
and this Gift of Self
in Love
is forever answered
by a return of
Love.

In the Triune God,
is Love giving itself,
losing itself and finding itself
in Love
and
Love returning to itself,
giving itself back
in Love.

This is the eternal pattern
of the universe.

306

In the depth of my Being
is a desire,
a longing for Love,
drawn by Love
to give myself
in Love.

This is the rhythm of the universe.

Every one of us
has in his/her heart
the desire to Love and be Loved.
It is the very structure of our
Being,
built into the cells of our bodies
and deepest instinct of our souls.

Sin is
a refusal to Love,
the rejection of the rhythm of Love,
a desire to get and not give.

God as Love
draws me through human Love
igniting me
to give myself
in Love
for the Love I have received.

Triune God:
Source of Love,
Love embodied,
Love enacted.

As written in I Jn 4, 7-16
When I Live in Love,
I Live in God,
and God in me.